To Reegie —
I enjoyed meeting you,
May happiness be with
you often!
Many Blessings,
[signature]

The

Pursuit

of

Happiness

Laurie Pond

ABOUT THE AUTHOR

David Pond (Washington) is an internationally recognized astrologer, author, speaker, and workshop leader. He and his wife, Laurie, lead groups to spiritual sites around the world and conduct workshops on integrating the chakras into daily life. A practicing professional astrologer since 1975, David has a master of science degree in experimental metaphysics from Central Washington University, which complements his lifelong spiritual practice of meditation and yoga. David has authored many books, including *Astrology & Relationships; Chakras for Beginners; Western Seeker, Eastern Paths; Mapping Your Romantic Relationships;* and, with his sister Lucy Pond, *The Metaphysical Handbook.*

The

Pursuit

of

Happiness

Integrating the Chakras
for Complete Harmony

DAVID POND

Llewellyn Publications
Woodbury, Minnesota

First Edition
First Printing, 2008

Cover design by Kevin R. Brown
Interior book design by Joanna Willis
Interior illustrations by Llewellyn art department

Llewellyn is a registered trademark of Llewellyn Worldwide, Ltd.

Library of Congress Cataloging-in-Publication Data
Pond, David.
  The pursuit of happiness: integrating the chakras for complete
harmony / David Pond.—1st ed.
    p. cm.
  ISBN 978-0-7387-1403-5
  1. Chakras—Miscellanea. 2. Happiness—Miscellanea. I. Title.
  BF1442.C53P67 2008
  294.5'43—dc22

                                                            2008031985

Llewellyn Publications
A Division of Llewellyn Worldwide, Ltd.
2143 Wooddale Drive, Dept. 978-0-7387-1403-5
Woodbury, MN 55125-2989, U.S.A.
www.llewellyn.com

Printed in the United States of America

To Bobby and his teaching:
"It's all about the love, man."

ALSO BY DAVID POND

Astrology & Relationships:
Techniques for Harmonious Personal Connections

Chakras for Beginners:
A Guide to Balancing Your Chakra Energies

Western Seeker, Eastern Paths:
Exploring Buddhism, Hinduism, Taoism & Tantra

Mapping Your Romantic Relationships:
Discover Your Love Potential

The Metaphysical Handbook
(coauthored with Lucy Pond)

CONTENTS

ACKNOWLEDGMENTS

I would like to thank Bobby, who inspired the writing of this book. He was a seeker looking for the meaning behind it all. Certainly my wife Laurie's heart, soul, and wisdom are in these pages; her careful editing and discussions about the material have helped immensely to bring the book to a coherent level. To the readers who painstakingly went through early copies and added their comments: Dave, Eden, Skylar, Forest, Patricia, Mike, Geri, Scott, Nimagna—thank you all. To Andria Friesen, whose insights and attention to every aspect of this book have proved to be invaluable. I would like to thank Carrie Obry from Llewellyn for contacting me and getting the ball rolling and then holding to her vision throughout the project. To be able to work with a good editor is a blessing, and Mindy Keskinen from Llewellyn has been just that. And to all the friends and seekers along the way who've shared a magical "aha" moment—your stories, our stories, are here.

I.

The

Dimensions

—— *of* ——

Being

INTRODUCTION

We humans are complicated beings, functioning and processing information on many levels. We need physical security, pleasure and accomplishment, a rich emotional life, self-expression, and mental and spiritual growth. No wonder life gets so confusing! Not only that, we live in changing times, and many people are feeling unsatisfied with the ways of life they grew up with.

We need something to help us sort it all out, to make sense of it all. That is the intention of this book. In these pages you will learn a clear method for regaining your authentic self and discovering the happiness that is always available to you. We all want happiness out of life; that is obvious enough. But I've learned that it cannot be sought directly. The pursuit of happiness is not a chase: it works from the inside out. Happiness arises naturally when our life works. Conversely, it's hard to be happy when our life isn't working.

In this book we will explore the seven levels of human happiness, each associated with a level of consciousness. As you examine your own life using the ideas and exercises here, you will become more authentic and more effective—and happier—in all aspects of your life. Most people know how to be happy in some areas of their lives, but not others. Some of us have learned to live with various combinations: these aspects of my life are satisfying; those are less so. With this book, you'll develop the skills to get your life working at all seven levels of consciousness.

Since these levels parallel the human chakra system, we will use that system as our gateway: it is the clearest, most universal model for understanding our levels of consciousness. But it is only a gateway. This book is experiential, not theoretical, and we will approach the chakras in a practical spirit, not an esoteric one. Whatever your previous knowledge of this ancient Indian wisdom, this book welcomes you. Life is multifaceted, and the chakra system gives us an organizing principle that helps us zero in on what is most important.

The seven chakras, or energy centers of the human self, govern seven key aspects of our being: the aspects that have to do with physical security, pleasure, power, heart, self-expression, mind, and spirit. These energy centers are absolutely universal. They do not depend on any religious or spiritual belief; they simply are. Readers of my earlier book *Chakras for Beginners* explored the meaning, location, and function of these energy centers. In this book we will apply those principles to experience greater happiness and harmony in all areas of life. It may sound like a lofty goal, but it is within reach, and these tools can help you live a more satisfying, fulfilling, loving, and spiritually meaningful life.

ENERGY FIRST

Of key importance in employing this system in your life is developing an "energy-first" approach. With this approach we deal with the energy animating a given experience, rather than the event itself. When you want to make changes in your life, instead of focusing on the outer issues, you first focus on your relationship to the energy of the experience. You learn that when you change that relationship, outer circumstances begin to fall into place. You first learn to reside in harmony within yourself—then the outer world coalesces around your energy and your world becomes harmonious.

A common example of experiencing energy that most of us can relate to is how we feel when we receive critical feedback. At first we feel like we've been kicked in the gut, and our energy field goes on the defensive. Energetically we are out of balance, and so are our thoughts and ideas. Any decisions or choices we make from this reactionary place will reflect that imbalance. When we work with an energy-first approach, we quell all reactions until we have come back to balance.

Take responsibility for getting your energy centered, *then* decide what to do with the feedback. Breathe and center yourself first, then you will be able to consider the criticism as information that you will choose to act on or not. Either way, you will be coming from your center and your decisions will reflect that balance.

THE WORLD IS CHANGING

We are in a transition age, born in a Pisces Age and evolving into the Aquarius Age. Pisces is an age of duality. Aquarius is an age of universality. We have been immersed in duality for 2,000 years: good against bad, upper chakras against lower chakras, my religion against your religion—a polarization that keeps us separate from ourselves. Trying to overcome evil, our lower selves, or whatever we call our enemy, casts us in an eternal battle that invariably empowers and perpetuates the very forces that we are trying to overcome, particularly within ourselves. To focus on something is to empower it, give it energy.

But we can learn a different way. We are moving from an era of separatism into an era of wholeness and synthesis.

The Reemergence of the Divine Feminine

If we look at the long arc of human history, it can be seen that we have been in a patriarchal era for nearly 5,000 years, an era in which God the father has reigned supreme, with worship and prayer the paths to invoke his benediction. But since at least the 1960s there has been a movement welcoming the return of the Divine Feminine. A growing number of people the world over are exploring a connection to the spiritual through the feminine path. Here, communion with the Divine is not so much worship and prayer to something external and distant; it is more of a celebration of co-creation.

The patriarchy has been aligned with the path of power: achievement, success, competition, and war are the name of the game. The Divine Feminine is the path of the heart, and as this movement continues, we will see more and more decisions made at all levels supporting quality of life for all. Imagine a world in which political decisions considered the path of the heart.

We have been immersed in an era of separatism, a constant battle within ourselves and with each other as to what is good and bad, right and wrong, and so on. The microcosm is reflected in the macrocosm; the battle within ourselves is reflected in our battles with each other. Living a life at all levels means coming to peace with yourself and accepting all aspects of your being without judgment: choosing a radical acceptance of who you are at the physical, emotional, mental, social, and spiritual levels, trusting in your direct experience, regaining your authentic self, and living a life of greater success, peace, and happiness. Then you learn to treat others with this same acceptance.

We need help with learning how to actually experience fulfillment and a sense of completeness. In the current status quo, we are taught to find our happiness by reaching for it externally. Get the right job, the right relationship, the right house, consume the right whatever, and you will be happy. We need to learn how to experience—not chase—happiness and fulfillment. That's what we'll do in this book: acknowledge the many aspects of your being, align them and get them working—so you can directly experience the happiness you've been chasing.

As we become familiar with the themes of each of our levels of being, we'll have more personal territory to explore, more insight to seek. Read about these seven levels and you will likely know specifically what is missing in your life and what you can do to move into a greater sense of wholeness in your life. As you learn to enter into balance at each of the levels, a deep sense of well-being comes over you—and happiness, once so elusive, becomes a more regular visitor.

THE MANY LEVELS
OF BEING

Life should be easier—and it would be if it weren't so complex! We must find our way at many levels, not just one. You are the one person experiencing it all, but your life is multidimensional. In this book, we will examine the seven levels of consciousness, which correspond with the seven levels of happiness: a sequence in which each level builds on the one that came before.

THE SEVEN LEVELS OF HAPPINESS

First let's look at the sequence as a whole, then we'll examine each level in detail.

1. The physical level, including your body and the material world

2. The pleasure level and the awakening of personal emotions

3. The power level and the drive to achieve

4. The heart level and all matters of love, from personal to universal

5. The expression level and the urge for creativity

6. The mental level, including your intuition and imagination

7. The spiritual level and that which feeds your soul and spirit

The first three levels support and sustain your life as a distinct individual. As you move into the upper levels, you move into the collective aspects of yourself, the aspects that are interconnected with all other forms of life. Your heart level is in the middle, linking your personal levels and your collective levels.

You are meant to live in harmony, and happiness is its measure. The more levels of your being you consciously experience, the richer your happiness becomes. True happiness is a guide, a barometer of your awareness of these levels. When you are balanced at any one level of your being, a natural happiness will result in that area. The trick is finding your way back to that which is already there. Natural happiness does not need to be achieved; it needs to be listened to. It is there, in the middle of all the chaos.

When you gain skill at mastering the energy at your many levels of being, your happiness is greatly expanded. A full life is all-inclusive; yes, even when you are awakened to the spiritual levels, you are still open to the joys and delights of being in a body—as well as to the perils and pitfalls.

The truth of your being is that you exist at all these levels simultaneously. In this book you will travel through each level, learning its territory and how it relates to your life. Each level has its delights and difficulties, and you will learn ways to spot where these issues are presenting themselves in your life. With each successive level, you expand, moving from a "me" focus to encompass a "we." To support this growth, you need a solid footing. Trying to build spiritual and collective levels on a shaky foundation has its obvious perils. If you are unbalanced in one of the lower levels, your life will be skewed to reflect this lack of balance. For example, if you fear for your basic physical security, soon everything seems frightful. The more you spend time in any state of consciousness, the more you attract experiences related to that state. The more time you spend feeling happy and fulfilled, the more happiness you attract. The more time you spend sad, frustrated, and angry, the more sad, frustrated, angry energy you attract.

So make sure your foundation is solid. Read the book through first for the big-picture view, if you wish, but in any case, work carefully through the seven levels in part 2, using the ideas and exercises in the order they are presented.

As we have noted, the pursuit of happiness is not a chase. The term implies that there is somewhere to go, whereas in truth there is nowhere to go. What you seek is already available. In fact, seeking a life of greater happiness and harmony will only lead to more seeking. You only have to experience it within yourself and then it unfolds naturally, as a blossoming of your inward state of balance and happiness.

This principle is contrary to our training. We expect guidance on what we should do to find happiness, to "get there." But the concept of "getting there" would take us right past where it is—in the here and now, the only place it can be.

TIPS FOR LIVING A MULTIDIMENSIONAL LIFE

To be skilled at living a full life, you need an elastic consciousness, one that can move freely from one level to another. To navigate the various currents of a multidimensional life, let's look at four points that greatly facilitate this mobility: the map, your Observer role, and the principles of balance and attention.

The Map

As we explore our territory—the seven levels of consciousness—you'll want a map. One good map can be found in the chakra system. It is worthwhile to contemplate your life and how each of your activities and interests fits within these energy centers. This can be particularly helpful when life seems overwhelming; tracking down the link between what is going on in your life and what chakra is being activated helps you clarify the issues.

For example, think of the confusion that commonly comes from thinking you are functioning on the mental level when you are actually processing information emotionally. Have you ever tried to have a rational argument over an emotional issue? It never works. Have anyone's feelings ever been changed by the argument that "it just doesn't make sense to feel that way"? You have to know how to tune in to the level that the issue is emanating from to effectively relate to it.

The first three levels—the physical, pleasure, and power levels—are the most personal, defining your own identity as distinct from others. Happiness at these levels is therefore more personal; your passion for life (first level), your delight in the senses (second level), and your exhilaration that comes from successes (third level). This is where you cultivate your taste, your style, and your interests. They have the strongest pull on your consciousness and it is easy to get immersed in life exclusively at these first three levels, but it never seems quite enough.

If you are focusing only on the material world, or the pursuit of pleasure or success, you will never get enough to satisfy yourself. These are all wonderful aspects of life, but they're not sufficient by themselves. That eternal hunger is satiated only when you awaken to the heart level and the practice of acceptance and gratitude. But you don't leave these personal levels behind. Even with the awakening of the heart, you still experience these personal levels as vital and compelling. They will still bring the life force, gusto, and passion to an integrated life. They will still have a grasping, doing, active quality. But you no longer have the illusion that as soon as you acquire or fix something, or attain a certain pleasure, then you will have achieved fulfillment. The hunger for life experiences never ends, but what *can* end is the illusion that as soon as all the petty issues are resolved, then you will be happy.

It's not that daily life is suddenly and miraculously free of difficulties. But as you become skilled at shifting gears throughout the day, you'll find that you can rise above even the tough times and shift your attention toward the rejuvenating spiritual dimensions of everyday life. You can't receive the benefit of the spiritual levels merely by knowing about them. You reap the rewards through regular contact with spirit with some type of activity aimed toward that intention. Creating some type of spiritual refuge gives you the opportunity to totally put down what you are carrying, take your mind out of gear, and be freshly renewed by your contact with spirit.

To live a life open to all levels is to be skillful in each and able to move harmoniously among them. When all seven are operating together, the energy creates synergistic activation—not just fulfillment as in contentment, but an activation of higher-level awareness. You awaken into solution-based consciousness, knowing that all issues are resolvable. You begin to see beyond dualistic thinking (good and bad) and start seeing from a unified field of consciousness with a larger perspective that includes all of the other views. Instead of *this or that* thinking, you move to *this and that too*.

Ideally, you want to be on friendly terms with all seven. You want to know your way around the territory—each of the levels on the map. But here's a question: if all the levels are aspects of you, who's doing the looking? Who can see all of these levels of life? This brings us to your Observer.

The Observer

Your Observer is the place within you that is detached from experiences and silently observes and notes what is going on. Developing a rapport with this part of your character is essential. To navigate, you first need to know where you are, and it is your Observer who knows the quality of your energy at any given time.

The Observer comes from the sixth level, the mental. We will explore that level thoroughly later, but we need to use this principle right away if we are to gain skill in moving from one level to another. Someone has to be watching the show. This is your Observer, the place within you that is simply witnessing and absorbing what is going on with you at all levels of life. Without your Observer, you could not learn from life experiences. It is the still, quiet voice within, the place your inner teachings come from. Most spiritual traditions refer to such a place, calling it by various names: the Witness, the Detached Observer, the Point of Mindfulness, or the Third Eye.

It is tremendously valuable to cultivate your ability to have your attention both in the moment and watching the moment. From the Observer point of view, you don't even judge yourself. As humans, we all have less than honorable parts of our character; your Observer even sees these neutrally. "To see with eyes unclouded by judgment" is spiritual guidance of the highest order, and seemingly impossible from our personality levels of being. You might find it easier in some settings than others; for example, it could be fairly easy in nature to simply see and observe the plants, flowers, and trees, and not judge what you are seeing. But it is considerably more difficult with people, and even harder to see yourself without judgment. But this Observer does exist within you, and you can learn to reside in the peace found beyond the analytical mind. The Observer within you knows where you are, which level you are operating on. This is where awareness is born. Whatever other levels you are working on, bring your Observer with you and you will grow in awareness.

Developing your Observer is essential; it is your main reference point for all energy work. You may want to read the section starting on page 172 to further develop your skills and confidence with this indispensable faculty.

Balance

As you develop your ability to move freely from one level to another, you will find balance essential. When your equilibrium is off-kilter at a particular level, you will attract other experiences of imbalance from this level, restricting your freedom. Equilibrium is a key to working with energy at any level.

When you master balance in your ability to handle life's situations, you attract harmony into your life. The idea seems almost too simple—by balancing your energy at whatever you are doing, you bring greater harmony into your life—but it is true! We usually go at it the other way around: do you wish that everything around you would come into balance first, so that you can then feel that cherished harmonious state of being? This is putting the cart before the horse! It will be better for you to simply learn how to feel balanced in any situation, and then watch how life coalesces around your state of being.

Balanced decisions are born from a stable place in your being. When you are off balance and take action to try to regain stability, you typically overcompensate and then have to make adjustments for that action, and on and on it goes. Better to do something to regain your center first. Then make decisions and take action. First, go for a walk, clear your head, regain clarity, then act.

Come to a place of balance within yourself first, then make important decisions. Following this one deceptively simple practice brings an amazing amount of peace and harmony into your life.

Activities for regaining this equilibrium are as varied as people are. There are many breathing techniques for centering yourself (see pages 158–160 for a few), but one very effective classic form simply consists of deep breathing with the intention of coming into balance. As you breathe, imagine drawing the centering strength of the earth up into your heart while simultaneously drawing the animating energy of spirit down from the heavens, through the crown of your head and into your heart. Center your attention in your heart and feel the balancing effect.

Of course balance can be found through numerous life activities as well: a walk or a workout, gardening, calligraphy, surrendering to the chores of everyday life, flower arranging, bringing beauty into any environment, listening to music, or almost anything else that you enjoy. The key is do what it takes to get balanced, then proceed.

Attention

Whichever level you are focusing on, where exactly is your attention? Taking responsibility for what you pay attention to, and seeing its importance in your life, is a key to growth. Where you direct your attention is something you do have control over, and it becomes one of your main resources in cultivating greater happiness. There are always two aspects to any experience you have. There is the event that you are taking part in, such as raking the backyard, and then there is the person experiencing it all—what you are experiencing within yourself as you clean the yard. The raking doesn't define your experience; it only defines the task. Are you happy, impatient, frustrated, or thankful that you even have a yard? Events happen, with or without your personal input. But where you are within yourself, and what you pay attention to—those are the parts of the equation that you do have more control over.

This simple saying, "What you pay attention to, grows," carries a huge truth within it. One of the greatest resources you have is your attention. "Pay attention" may sound like a clichéd phrase, but it offers a great wisdom! Your attention is your navigational system for moving around in the many levels of reality. When you invest your attention, you direct your life force. When you pay attention to something you don't like, you are directing your life force toward that which you don't want! Knowing that this is your investment, you would wisely redirect your attention to something you want to see grow.

This is especially important with relationships of all types. If you spend too much time thinking about what you don't like about the other person, it often seems to magnify the issue; it grows and grows. In this circumstance it would be wise to take some of that energy and focus your thoughts on what you *do* like about the other person and how you would like your relationship to improve. You would be investing your thoughts into something that can make a positive difference in a relationship.

Paying attention to your inner self-talk is where you do the real work of making change toward happiness in your life. Where does your mind drift to when you are not directing it? What is the quality, the tone, the temperament of these thoughts? Pay attention to what your mind is paying attention to. If these thoughts are truly creating tomorrow's reality, are they worthy of you? Is this really how you choose to script your life? How you think about life is something you do have control over. You can learn to employ it as one of your main tools for experiencing greater happiness.

It is wise to begin your day with affirmations, a statement of intention, asking for grace, or some other method of setting your compass. But it is in monitoring your inner self-chatter throughout the day that you do the real work of changing your thinking patterns. Monitoring yourself in this way allows you to make the subtle course corrections to follow through on your intended path.

As you define yourself, so your life becomes. You define yourself by what you actually think about throughout the day.

Of all that there is to be known and experienced, what did you choose to invest yourself into today? Use your Observer to catch yourself when you drift to undesirable places. Realize this is something you have direct control over. Life is short. Start now—not sometime in the future when the circumstances will be right.

LIFE IS HOW YOU LOOK AT IT

Much of our experience of life is based on how we look at it. Life coalesces around our perception. Attitude is everything. Learning how to shift your definitions of happiness and framing experiences in a positive light will lead to a marked improvement in your capacity to experience happiness. Whatever human consciousness looks for, it finds. Scientists are discovering this at the level of quantum physics. You can't separate the observer from the effect; what the observer is looking for influences the behavior of what is being observed. The life lesson for us is to understand the manifesting power of our attention: learn to look for happiness, and this is what you will find.

Modern science is becoming as mystical as mysticism! Discoveries in neuroscience have revealed a principle known popularly as "wiring is firing." The idea is that the more often you think a specific thought or have a particular reaction, the more deeply you are etching a physical pathway in the brain, ensuring the continuance of the pattern. By continually thinking a particular thought, you are literally creating the wiring in your brain to sustain this activity.

To change the wiring, change the firing. By stopping your thinking about something, you unplug the life force of your attention. The brain wiring that continually brings the material up begins to disappear. Redirect your thoughts toward something healthy, and the wiring will be created to support the activity. The physical wiring of our brain coalesces around what we think about. Change your thoughts, and your brain circuitry changes!

The message is this: mastering our ability to direct our attention to what we choose can have more impact on the quality of our life than any other personal resource. The same sun rises and sets on all of us. It is what we pay attention to that defines our unique experience.

THE CHAKRA SYSTEM: A GATEWAY TO THE SEVEN LEVELS OF HAPPINESS

As we have noted, this book's seven levels of happiness parallel the human chakra system. First described in ancient Indian writings, this system offers a timeless view of the seven "energy centers" that govern our health and growth.

While this system is very useful to our understanding for our current work, a thorough knowledge of it is not essential. Readers who are already familiar with the chakras, or who wish to move to the more direct discussion of human happiness, can easily skip this chapter. But I hope that those who do read this brief section will find a simple, practical introduction to a tool that can greatly enhance their self-exploration.

The chakras provide a precise map to the human energy system and seven distinct levels of consciousness. This is the energy blueprint for the human operating system. To know your chakras is to know how you are meant to operate at optimum, and to know precisely which chakra is out of balance when your energy system is out of whack.

Chakra	Drive	Core Issue	Perspective	Level of Consciousness	Sign of Imbalance	Task
1	*survival*	find place on earth	animal instinct; separate sense of self	safety; connection to body and earth	insecurity	to be fully in the body
2	*pleasure*	explore sensuality/sexuality	emotional self	awareness of magnetic energy	hedonism; self-indulgence	to enjoy life
3	*power*	exercise willpower; initiate activities and set boundaries	principles; what you stand for	seeking opportunities to assert will	power conflicts	to learn to choose wisely
4	*love*	open heart to all; take a noncompetitive approach	cooperation	being at peace	bleeding heart	to experience joy
5	*creativity*	speak your truth	unique worldview beyond cultural conditioning	observing without bias, then synthesizing varying views	inability to express yourself	to be authentic
6	*transcendence*	inspire others	transcending polarities through insight	gaining intuitive guidance by aligning with larger reality	spacing out; illusions	to direct imagination
7	*spirituality*	connect with Divine intent	seeing through the eyes of the Divine	experiencing all of life as spiritual	"shopping list" mentality	to surrender

24

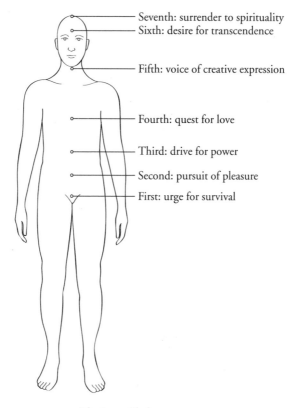

Seventh: surrender to spirituality
Sixth: desire for transcendence

Fifth: voice of creative expression

Fourth: quest for love

Third: drive for power

Second: pursuit of pleasure

First: urge for survival

The Seven Chakras

The word *chakra* means "spinning wheel," and indeed, a chakra can be perceived as a vortex of energy. There are seven main chakras aligned in front of the spine from the tailbone to the crown of the head. They are not physical; they are energetic—and each one governs a particular aspect of the human experience, from the instinctual to the refined.

All human beings have all seven chakras, although they may function decidedly differently in different people. They are our connection to the universal life force. They store and distribute the universal energy to animate our life activities. From the most physical activities to the subtlest of meditations, the chakras have a direct role. Although our chakras may be developed (or undeveloped) to various degrees, they are never fully blocked—that is, not if we are alive!

The chakras are not only centers of energy; they are the seven distinct levels of consciousness. Each chakra gives us a different outlook on life; traveling the chakras is like riding an elevator to the various floors in a building. The chakras are a map to all the "floors" of our levels of consciousness. Studying them can help us see when we are stuck viewing life from a given floor, thinking that this is all of reality. The chakra map shows the way out of conflict with life and points the way to live in harmony, in touch with our innate creativity and aligned with inner guidance.

Balance is the key to working with the chakras. When the energy is balanced at a particular chakra, it naturally rises to the next. It's not as if you have to push the energy to the upper chakras; with equilibrium it naturally happens. Imbalances attract situations that demand your attention at the imbalanced chakra; for now, your consciousness is limited to the chakra demanding attention. As you bring the energy back into balance, it naturally rises on its own.

As we noted earlier, the lower three chakras drive the needs of your personal self. The fourth chakra awakens you to the needs of the your soul. The upper chakras animate your connection to collective and spiritual levels of consciousness. This is the energetic dance of the body, soul, and spirit, which ideally all interact, supporting and enriching each other. Energy moves freely through all chakras when they are balanced within themselves and each other.

FIRST CHAKRA:
THE URGE FOR SURVIVAL

At the base of your spine is the first or root chakra, your deepest connection to your animal nature and instincts for survival. This vital life force runs though your body and brings passion and excitement for being alive. When the first chakra is balanced, you feel secure; when imbalanced, you feel insecurity and fear. For a balanced first chakra, it is important to have found your right place on the earth, a place that revitalizes your body and sense of well-being. If you walk out your door in the morning and the environment itself, the climate, vegetation, and the feel of the land revitalizes you, you are there.

You can't create security; you have to feel it and enter into it. Learn to trust that you are part of the universal life force expressed through all of nature, and that you are meant to be here. You are part of the fabric of nature, not separate from it. Know that you are sustained by the same life force that animates all of nature. Your instincts are strong with this balance. Fear is like a smoke alarm, on standby and ready to report danger, but not always sounding. When the first chakra is not balanced, you can feel insecure, ungrounded and out of touch with your body. If you are locked in fear, find small ways to embrace life so you can ease out of the threatened place. Pet an animal, commune with a tree, or find counsel with a mountain stream. These can help break the illusion of feeling separate and isolated from life.

To activate your first chakra, get physical as best you can. From exercise to chores, activate the body. Connect with the earth through walking, hiking, gardening, stacking firewood, or whatever works for you. One way or another, feel the revitalizing impact on your first chakra that a connection to the earth brings to you.

SECOND CHAKRA:
THE PURSUIT OF PLEASURE

Your second chakra is located in your lower abdomen, just above your pubic bone. With an awakened second chakra, surviving is not enough—you want to enjoy your life and the sensory world. This is the chakra of pleasure and delight of the senses, of sexuality and sensuality. Great happiness is found in your second chakra through the ability to appreciate beauty, to enjoy the embrace of love, to taste the sweet taste of fruit or the luxury of chocolate. Yes, life without an awakened second chakra would be bland and lacking of joy. But the quest for pleasure can be never-ending until one has truly learned to enter into the pleasure and not simply chase it.

A balanced second chakra is the sweet kiss of life. You know how to enjoy life's simple pleasures and have learned how to express this enjoyment in many ways. You are not attached to any one source for enjoying life. With an awakened second chakra, you take the skill wherever you go and voilà!

Life's enjoyable wherever you are. You have learned how to appreciate and enjoy sensory experiences without grasping for more. Instead of chasing pleasure, you experience it, by bringing gratification right to the core of your being. A balanced second chakra could be described by the saying, "To experience more joy in your life, spend more time wanting what you have and less time wanting what you don't have."

When the second chakra is not balanced, too much or too little focus on pleasure can result. To restore balance, cultivate your capacity to enjoy life's simple pleasures. This allows you to experience deeper satisfaction, and the illusion of needing more or less is broken. When you experience something enjoyable, cultivate the ability to appreciate that enjoyment; linger in that experience rather than reaching for more—and you are there.

THIRD CHAKRA:
THE DRIVE FOR POWER

Your third chakra is located at your solar plexus, just above your navel. Here you awaken to issues concerning power. A balanced third chakra brings the effective use of willpower. You know how to say no when you mean no, and yes when you mean yes. You feel you have some control over your life; you have confidence that you can act on your plans and initiate activity. You have learned how to take charge of a situation, if that is what is required, and how to back off when appropriate. Your power is not just in external issues; more importantly, you have developed self-control, and an effective life is the result.

When the third chakra is not balanced, issues surface concerning willpower, either too much or too little. The surest way to maintain balance in the third chakra is to practice some self-discipline. In small ways or big ways, demonstrate some self-control. Establish a healthy schedule and stick to it; set some goals for yourself or initiate a fitness routine; practice restraint somewhere in your life just to demonstrate to yourself that you can! Effectiveness begins at home. When you begin to focus more on self-control than on expressing frustration with events or others, the agitating experiences begin to diminish, and happiness grows.

FOURTH CHAKRA:
THE QUEST FOR LOVE

Your fourth chakra is located in the center of your chest at the level of your heart. When all three of the lower chakras are balanced, the energy naturally rises here, to the heart chakra. This is both a quantum leap and a qualitative shift of where you direct your attention. You rise above petty issues and experience the joy of deep acceptance. From the awakened heart, life no longer seems threatening, nor a struggle. Competition gives way to cooperation. Anxiety gives way to tranquility. Hostility gives way to love. Whether it is experienced as personal love, compassionate love, or universal love, it is always unconditional: you have learned how to tap into a source of love that is not dependent on circumstances, nor on how others treat you.

The heart chakra is the first of the upper chakras, where you tap into universal energy. When you share and give from the awakened heart, the love comes through you; you are tapping into the universal, inexhaustible source and you will not experience the burnout and exhaustion that comes from personal giving.

When imbalances occur with any of the upper chakras, the cause is most likely a lower-chakra disruption that is deflecting the true course of the chakra in question. With the heart chakra, troubles in love have their source in issues of security, pleasure, or power that interfere with your attention to the heart. To balance these issues, go to the source chakra, restore equilibrium there, and then you will be able to reside more regularly in your heart.

Even with compassion, "I suffer for you" brings it all back to the "I," the realm of the lower chakras. The separate "I" melts with the awakened heart and it becomes possible to gently touch suffering with loving kindness and not carry the suffering with you. Joy is a function of immense acceptance. This is certainly referring to an awakened heart. To stay centered in your heart, practice deep acceptance by dropping all judgments of self and others. Even excessive humility ("I'm not worthy") and despair ("Woe is me") are still focused on "I" and "me." When judgment happens, note it, recognize it as the voice of the lower chakras, and simply decide not to listen to the judgment, not to empower it in any way. This helps you to literally rise above the petty voices and stay centered in your loving and accepting heart.

FIFTH CHAKRA:
THE VOICE OF CREATIVE EXPRESSION

As the energy rises to the fifth chakra at your throat, you awaken to original insights and can creatively express yourself in a way that is not conditioned by culture or others. You find your true voice. At this level you are seeking freedom of expression, not just in what you say but in what you think. You become interested in the innovative, the original, and authentic in all concerns. Your ability to express yourself creatively comes from this access to the source of all human creativity. Here in the upper chakras, you connect with the universal, collective mind through insights and sudden knowing.

This common scenario shows that the fifth chakra is collective, not personal, in nature: Imagine that you have a creative inspiration, but for one reason or another you fail to act on it. What happens? Somebody else writes your book, or your play, or comes up with the invention, or acts on the original insight that you thought was yours. Creativity is a collective resource; if you don't act on your creative inspirations, somebody else will.

Liberating yourself from all cultural conditioning facilitates the awakening of your fifth chakra. Those who can sustain a fifth-chakra level of awareness are universal in their perspective of truth. By rising out of your own conditioning you are able to see the beauty behind many religions, beliefs, and political views. You become like an evolutionary agent for your culture, and your insights serve as a catalyst for others to question their views as well.

A nervous type of energy accompanies opening of the fifth chakra. When you try to quell this energy, it is experienced as nervous anxiety; when you align with it, it is sensed as a quickening. Imbalances in the fifth, such as writer's block, or inability to speak up in a group, or stage fright, all stem from the ego inappropriately identifying with energy it can't control. Keep the ego and lower chakras out of it. If you allow yourself to offer your piece of the puzzle, your fifth chakra will operate at its best.

SIXTH CHAKRA: THE DESIRE FOR TRANSCENDENCE

The sixth chakra is located behind the brow, just above the bridge of the nose. As the energy rises here, your Third Eye is awakened and inner vision is born with imagination as its mode of expression. The ability to see with your eyes closed, to imagine experiences that are not available to your normal sensory world—this is truly a gift. From the sixth-chakra perspective, you rise above all polarity in your life and see a larger reality that encompasses all duality. This is the home of the Observer consciousness that regards the self in action. You are in the world but not of the world; thus you are not pulled into polarities.

This is the realm of the angels, ascended beings, the flow of the Tao, the Big Sky mind, and the still, quiet voice within; experiences from a balanced sixth chakra are always inspirational. When you are aligned with it, your faith in the source beyond self is empowered by direct experience, and a sense of knowing beyond mental concepts comes over you.

When the pure witnessing of the balanced sixth chakra is disturbed by the desires and fears of the lower chakras, this spiritual faculty gets deflected to the ego's needs and fears. When the imagination is linked to creative, mystical, and spiritual sources, your energy field is always enhanced.

Whether it was inspiration or illusion that you have been listening to is always evident retrospectively. It is only too clear after the fact. To catch your imagination in the moment and notice if it is moving toward inspiration or illusion is subtle work, but it is profound. If I asked you to take notice of your general energy field while you were reading this passage, you could easily do this, noting whether you were feeling inspired, tired, agitated, or other feelings. The place within you that is doing the noticing is the Observer. The key is to do this very same assessment while in the state of imagination.

To work with your sixth chakra, you need to know that fear and faith are flip sides of the same coin. They are both fueled by the imagination, but have radically different impacts on your energy field. When you hear a noise outside your room and fear it might be an intruder, your energy field responds quite differently than if you imagined the noise to be a reminder from your guardian angel. It takes your spiritual will to (1) stay observant to whether your imagination is moving toward fear or faith, and (2) extract your attention from negative wanderings and direct it to that which inspires you.

SEVENTH CHAKRA:
THE SURRENDER TO SPIRITUALITY

When the energy rises to the crown of the head and the seventh chakra, you become absorbed into spiritual consciousness. The crown chakra is also called the "thousand-petaled lotus blossom" because it represents the flowering of human consciousness at its highest expression, yet its roots are deep in the muck of reality. Here all sense of separate identity dissolves into the vast Oneness of life. Only a handful of saints and masters have been able to sustain this level of consciousness, while for most of us, there will only be a few glimpses of this reality in an entire lifetime. Psychologists have talked of "peak" or "oceanic" experiences that, although rare, often mark major transitions in a person's life. These openings of the seventh chakra are glimpses of life through God's eyes.

Seventh-chakra experiences are ineffable; they can't be described. "The tao that can be told is not the eternal Tao."* This is the realm of enlightenment and God-centered consciousness. If you are so blessed as to receive a few of these illuminating experiences in this life, don't try to understand them with your mind, just be thankful that you have been so blessed. To open to this energy, practice quieting your mind and noticing the God force that is all around you. Open to this divine energy and picture receiving it into your being through your crown chakra.

---

*Stephen Mitchell, *Tao Te Ching* (New York: HarperPerennial, 1992), 3.

A CHAKRA MEDITATION

Sit in a comfortable meditation position with your spine straight. Align your head directly over your shoulders, not slouched forward. You can imagine a cord attached to the crown of your head that is gently pulling you upward. Take a few deep breaths to center yourself. Let a gentle smile come over your face and feel the warmth of simply smiling. As you inhale the colors in the following exercise, breathe in a smile along with the colors and let it wash over your whole body.

Now imagine the color red in your mind's eye—any shade of red that comes to you will work. Imagine inhaling this color on a deep in-breath. Bring it all the way down to your tailbone. As you hold your breath, focus your attention on your first chakra and picture the red energy animating your being. Imagine the chakra as a wheel of red light, spinning and radiating and filling you with this hue. Feel the courage and strength of red animate your body. Here you are a creature of nature, part of the animal kingdom. Feel the aliveness of your body and imagine being at the place on earth where your body absolutely feels its best. Here, you can trust your instincts for survival and trust that you will be safe and cared for on the earth this day. Feel the security come over you; empower your first chakra with trust.

Now imagine any shade of orange that comes to your mind. Breathe in orange and pull it down to your second chakra, just above the pubic bone. As you focus there, picture this spinning and radiating orange light. Feel the joy, the warmth, and the pleasure of awakening your second chakra. Know that you are a magnetic being and can attract to you all you need and want. As you breathe out, send this joyous, magnetic energy out into the world.

Next is yellow and the third chakra. Again, find the shade of yellow that you are drawn to, and breathe this color into your solar plexus chakra, just above your navel. As you inhale, see the chakra begin to spin and radiate yellow. Feel the power of your will, and know that you can use your will wisely. From here you can initiate activities and define your boundaries. Feel the confidence that comes from having self-control, from knowing you can say yes when you mean yes and no when you mean no.

On to the fourth chakra and the color green (some experience this as pink). Find a shade that calls to you in your mind's eye, and breathe this color into your heart chakra in the middle of your chest. Set the chakra spinning and radiating a green light that fills your entire being. Rest in the healing energy of green. The heart chakra is the heaven-on-earth place, the meeting place of the lower and upper chakras. Feel the deep peace, joy, love, and compassion that arise with this awakening. When you look at others from your heart, you do not see their personality traits; you see another soul in a human incarnation struggling to be free. Compassion, empathy, and contentment are also experiences you can awaken to while centered here. It is particularly important to offer these experiences of love into the world. Establish the high intent that you will offer out into the world any good that comes from your meditation, so that it may be helpful to others.

Next move on to the fifth chakra and the color sky blue. Imagine looking up at the bright blue heavens. Breathe in this color and pull it down to the base of your spine. As the blue rises up your spine, feel it lengthen, as if a puff of air were floating between each of your vertebrae. Focus the blue on your throat chakra and set it spinning in your mind's eye. Feel yourself become as expansive as the sky. Here your thoughts become clear, unclouded by desires or the opinions of others. Here you breathe the same air that has animated all creative genius. Here you can speak the truth that does not need to be defended. Feel the freedom of your liberated mind as it sails into the sky, far removed from personal opinions—yours or others'. Pledging your intention to somehow help others with any information you might receive, be open to sudden knowing.

The sixth chakra and deep indigo blue come next. Imagine the color of the furthest reaches of Earth's atmosphere just before it turns black. Breathe this color into your Third Eye, just above the bridge of your nose. Again, imagine the chakra spinning and radiating this deepest of blue hues. Imagine yourself rising into the indigo atmosphere above Earth and looking back at the planet as if from a spacecraft. Feel the transcendence of this view. Your view is so far removed that you can't even see individual lives, only Earth and her continents, oceans, and weather. Feel the bliss of this transcendence. Allow the sacredness of the moment to wash over you. To stay centered here requires quieting the analytical voice. Just listen and observe. Thinking will happen, but pay it no mind—let the thoughts come and go as you stay anchored in your sixth chakra, simply observing. If any spontaneous devotional feelings for teachers, masters, or saints come over you while meditating on your sixth chakra, surrender to those feelings. Find the place of trust and faith that all of life is unfolding as it should.

The seventh chakra and the color violet complete the meditation. This is the most spiritual chakra, your connection to that which is most high. Imagine a violet flame over your head: deep violet where it touches your head and, as it rises into the heavens, increasingly ultraviolet and finally invisible. Deeply breathe in this spiritual flame and pull it down to the base of your spine. Picture it cleansing and purifying each chakra as it passes through. Now picture it rising again through each chakra and ultimately out your crown and up to the heavens. Focus your attention on your crown chakra and affirm, "I am a child of the Divine." Know that beyond all illusions and appearances you have a direct connection to the God/Goddess within. Here resides your eternal self, who has never been wounded or bruised by life. Feel as if you are being absorbed back into the One.

II.

The

Seven Levels

——— *of* ———

Happiness

ONE:
THE PHYSICAL LEVEL
OF HAPPINESS

Your life is an act of grace and a response to a set of needs that brought you here. You are part of nature, and all of nature is part of a vast web of interrelated needs. You discover your purpose by accepting your place in the natural order of things. The skills, talents, and abilities that you came to develop are brought out of you as you tend to the needs to which you are drawn.

Chakra: First (root chakra)—base of the spine.

Color: Red.

Core issues: The need to survive and thrive. Your physical body and its needs, including finding the right place on the earth for you to thrive.

Signs of imbalance: Fearfulness. Excessive concern with security. Insensitivity to others' needs. Coarseness. Overattachment to possessions.

Signs of balance: You are comfortable and enjoy being in your body. You feel secure and grounded on the earth and feel a reverence for all life. You have found a way to provide for yourself that is consistent with your true nature. You are passionate and honor your body's instincts.

Life lives! Imagine you're driving on a highway through a steep rock-walled river canyon. As you look at the rock wall, you notice a lone shrub growing right out of it, many feet up from the ground. The tenacity of life demonstrated by this lone shrub, thriving on who knows what—this is the throb of existence coursing through all of life, including us humans. In its purest form, the physical level is the innocent joy of being alive. Children are the best at this; they sometimes squeal with delight for no other reason than simply being alive! This passion for life and the excitement of the senses are the happiness of the physical level. Here you are acutely aware of the immediacy of life in front of you

You are in a body. This is Earth. The need is to survive, thrive, and feel secure. Your resources are your passions and instincts. Simple enough truths to start from. The physical level calls for being at ease in your body and tending to your physical needs for food, clothing, shelter, and livelihood. At this level you are most separate from all others; you view life from within the boundaries of a skin-encapsulated being.

Your physical body is the host for this experience of your life on Earth. Yes, you're more than just your body, but you do indeed have one, and you dwell within it. If healthy and vibrant, your body is a source of wondrous delight. If ill or wounded, its pain cannot be ignored. It gives you the most immediate and direct experience of life through the senses; life is happening, and your senses verify this. Because of this immediacy it is easy for the self-identity to anchor itself here. It is readily verifiable, hardcore reality.

FROM SEPARATENESS TO WHOLENESS

We can change our world and our lives not by becoming more spiritual but by expanding our concept of what spiritual is. Where is not God?

Religions in the age of separatism have inadvertently helped foster an attitude that being here on Earth might not be so great. Many teach that if you are really good, you'll get to a paradise that is not here and you won't have to come back to this less-than-desirable place. What does this imply about life here on planet Earth? Can we be surprised that humanity does not treat Earth as sacred, when so many of our teachings tell us that sacred is somewhere else?

We needn't negate the physical world to find the spiritual; they are woven from the same light. How would it be different if we treated the body and the planet as sacred? What if the cosmic joke turns out to be that Earth is the jewel of the entire system? That those who are here have not fallen from Divine grace, but have received Divine grace? How would that change the way we live on the planet?

We desperately need to return to a sacred awareness of the body and the gift of life. If we learn to respect the life coursing through our own veins, we can learn to respect the same life flowing through the veins of our fellow humans and all of life. Inhabiting a body links us genetically to all other beings of the same species. That which is going on within the body of humanity is going on within each of us. The lack of respect for life itself that our species demonstrates can be seen in the number of people for whom survival is a daily challenge, not just a metaphor. If we had respect for all life as our core fundamental belief, this wouldn't be so. We would never allow political or economic considerations to overshadow the basic human right for food and survival for anyone.

Earth is a paradise for us to steward for future generations of us to enjoy. What if we were raised to believe that our life itself is a response to the needs that brought each of us here? It is exhausting to believe that we have to impose ourself on life, to somehow or another "make it." How different is the belief that our own natural skills, talents, abilities, and interests are perfect for fulfilling the needs we came to serve. What if we raised our children to believe that our lives are part of a vast interconnected web, and that this life is an act of grace?

SECURITY

One spinoff of the survival instinct is concern about security; thus all issues of security stem from the physical level of experience. It is easy to get caught up in chasing security as if it were a carrot dangled in front of a donkey: we never quite attain it, but we're always reaching for it. When we are in healthy alignment with our physical level of being, we enter into the feelings of security rather than chasing them. We live with assurance that our skills, talents, and abilities are plenty adequate to meet all of our needs.

EXERCISE FOR EXPERIENCING SECURITY

Here's an exercise that can directly alleviate feelings of insecurity. When your bills have got you down, go out into nature and try this activity. Your backyard or the park will do. First, simply observe nature. Notice how inexhaustible the life force is, animating all of the plants, insects, birds, and trees. Now move from the observing role into a more experiential one, and begin to sense this same life force moving through you and all of life. The birds have no day-to-day guarantee of finding a worm; they simply live each moment within the fabric of nature and survive. You are more than just watching now. You begin to feel that you are part of this same fabric of nature, and it is as if life is living you as much as you are living life! Let this sweet wave of security wash over you.

As you go back to your stack of paperwork, your bills aren't any more paid than they were before, but you feel less neurotic about them! Are you secure in this moment? Is there a roof over your head? Enough to eat? Is there some beauty around to enjoy? Enter into the enjoyment of this security—that's what is real in this moment. You have to make something up in your head for it to get worse, or for you to be insecure.

Right Livelihood

We all need to get by at minimum, or find meaningful work if we're lucky. This leads to the question of right livelihood. Ideally, the right way to provide for yourself meets all three of these criteria:

1. A livelihood you can **enjoy**

2. A livelihood that utilizes your **unique skills**

3. A livelihood that meets a **need** in the world

Since your work is going to be such a major portion of your life activity, make sure it is more than just a job. Find something that holds your natural interest. When you engage in the type of work that you actually enjoy and can put your heart into, of course it makes all the difference in the world in terms of happiness. The second point is obvious enough as well: you have to be sufficiently skilled for others to want what you have to offer. You can love all types of activities that you might not be good enough at to get paid. I love to golf, but I'm not all that good at it. The question of right livelihood will involve using your genuine and unique skills in a practical context.

The third point is to find a livelihood that not only serves a true need in the world, but also goes beyond charitable activity. You interact with the needs that you are genuinely drawn to. The needs carry a vortex of energy with them that you can draw upon to meet them. Essentially, you are forming a relationship with the needs. Instead of imposing yourself on the tasks, you enter into a relationship with the needs, and they are met through you. Within this meeting is where you find right livelihood.

I have seen the impact of this teaching on those in the helping professions. Burnout is an occupational hazard from giving, giving, giving. Some counselors are totally spent after seeing three clients a day, yet others see six or more as a matter of a day's work and seemingly can go on doing this indefinitely. The burnout candidates typically give everything of themselves until there is nothing left. The energy is moving in one way. Those who thrive in the giving professions have learned to surrender into the needs of the task in front of them, trusting that the needs essentially draw out the skills necessary to meet them. The task gets done through them, not from them. The energy flows two ways in this type of interaction, and these counselors (and teachers, nurses, waiters, sales clerks, and so on) often gain valuable insights about themselves and life while interacting with others.

As the provider for my family, I have worked with this principle of responding to needs rather than simply doing tasks. When the fear of not being able to provide for everyone's needs creeps in, I take the attitude that "nature will provide." I assume that a power that can create this entire universe isn't going to have difficulty providing for my family and our needs. I trust that as the provider for my family, their needs for me to do this will draw the skills and talents out of me to provide for them.

I'm reminded of a Native American teaching: "Children come with their own breadbasket." It is nature's way: since children can't provide for themselves, their support is drawn through their providers. We don't have to just give the provisions, we can take part in nature's way working through us. With this attitude, providing for children is the opposite of a handicap. Instead, it allows us to rise to those needs, bringing the skills, talents, and abilities out of us to meet them.

Survival and Instincts

Your physical level is where you have to stand up for yourself. And of course if you're not able to stand up for yourself, the rest of your life is built on questionable foundations. You have to create a life that is natural for you, that is born out of your natural way of being. Otherwise, you are fighting yourself right from the start in your pursuit of a fulfilling life. You have to know enough about yourself to decide whether you're a city or country type of person. Do you thrive on a busy life or quiet life? Do you thrive in the presence of others or by yourself?

The physical level of consciousness speaks to you through your instincts. This body-based wisdom is pre-mental and is the wisdom of the species encoded within you. Your gene pool is the repository of a very long line of ancestors who also worked on their survival skills. This inherited wisdom is encoded within your body. Honor it. Keep it fit. Listen to its intelligence, and it will reward you with spontaneous action when required.

I have experienced strange events that have utterly confirmed to me the instinctual intelligence of the body. I'm no superman, but on one occasion I tapped into powers that amaze me still.

I was visiting my mother-in-law in her new home at the edge of a golf course, part of a development that was still under construction with trucks and heavy equipment in evidence. We were all chatting in the family room when a huge explosion rocked the house. My body immediately jumped up and ran toward the door. This and the ensuing events all happened without my conscious volition; my body was simply moving on its own accord. As I reached the door, I could see a truck engulfed in a fiery inferno. I found myself sprinting across the golf course toward a point in the woods about a hundred yards beyond the burning truck. I was very aware that my body was moving without my guidance.

It was then that I noticed a child running through the woods totally engulfed in flames, and that my body was running directly toward the child-comet. I jumped on the young boy and rolled him in the mud to extinguish the blaze, then picked him up and carried him to the house. The fire department's emergency response vehicle was there in no time and whisked the child to the hospital.

The boy had been playing near the construction vehicles and dropped a lit match down the truck's gas tank to see what would happen. He was badly burned from the explosion, but was able to eventually regain full movement of his body.

Although this was a rare experience in my life, stories like this are not uncommon, and they remind us that the body has an intelligence of its own—instincts. Athletes know instincts well; their bodies are trained to respond without thought. Learn to cultivate your animal wisdom by keeping your body vital.

Your Place on the Earth

Your physical level of being is that which connects you to the earth and has much to do with where you feel best about living. You know you're in the right place if, when you step outside in the morning and breathe the air, you feel sustained by the environment: the climate, the vegetation, the atmosphere, all feel just right. Welcome home; this is a right and perfect place for you.

It's trickier when you don't feel connected to the geographical area where you live. You never seem to take root and thrive. When this is the situation, you don't quite click with the feeling of being in the right place. Ideally, you would move to an area that your being thrives in. Short of that, it's imperative to find some place in nature where you do feel connected and energized. It can be your backyard, or a park, or a small garden—find your spot and visit it regularly. You can also do a very physical activity: go to the gym and pump iron, dig in the earth, run, or do yoga. These types of activities help you feel grounded in the body, if not sore! Find a place or activity that generates a smile. Consciously absorb this energy to draw on later.

A HOUSE-CLEANSING CEREMONY

Houses have memories and hold energy, some more than others, and it is wise when moving into a previously occupied house, particularly older homes with lots of history, to perform a house-cleansing ceremony. Sometimes houses and buildings hold energy that is incongruous to your sense of well-being, and this can contribute to feelings of insecurity on the physical level.

Many cultural traditions have housecleaning ceremonies—such as throwing salt in the corners, opening all the windows and doors and sweeping energy out of a building, burning candles, incense, and sage—so there is no single right way to do this. It is the spirit of the intent that is important; then you add some ritual to empower the intent. The following is a favorite of my household's. It is inspired by the Celtic tradition but can be adapted as the spirit moves. This ceremony could also be used to clear offices, buildings, and businesses.

You can do this by yourself or with one or more people. You will go through the entire house several times, first chasing out any lingering spirits and then inviting in the protective spirits of your choice.

Start inside the main entrance door to your home. Move along the entire inside perimeter, beating a drum or pots and pans, or shaking a rattle or other percussion instruments, while shouting, "Spirits be gone!" Make it a rather noisy affair. Walk along the inside of every wall and every room while drumming and shouting. After completing one cycle, do another around the whole perimeter, this time carrying burning sage and a bowl of saltwater. Pay particular attention to each corner and doorway, sprinkling it with saltwater and blessing it with some extra smoke from the smudge stick, this time chanting in a more friendly tone, "Spirits, we honor you and bless you and send you on your way."

Now make a third trip around the perimeter. This time, dance and sing in your most lighthearted way to welcome in your protective spirits, saying, "May all those who enter here feel safe and at home," "May the spirits who guide me to my highest calling be welcome here," or a variation that fits your inclination. On this third trip, you celebrate your home and welcome in your supporting guides, spirits, and angels.

Afterward, consider placing a pair of special stones, such as rose quartz rocks, outside every entrance door to your home. Place one on each side to signify protection and to convey that all who enter will receive the blessing.

FEAR

Fear comes from the physical level, and is another spinoff of the survival instinct, part of its system. Fear has its function; it is useful, for example, when you instinctively pull back to avoid a snake on the path in front of you. If fear is not overwhelming, but rather a call not to fail at a given task, it can even prod you to your highest achievements.

Fear is useful when it serves as a smoke alarm—a signal that is latent until it is required. Such an alarm is useful because it isn't *always* sounding its signal of distress. When it does sound, you know there is something to pay attention to. If a smoke alarm were sounding all the time, it would be absolutely useless. If a smoke alarm sounded in a building we were in, we would exit right away. But if every time we entered the building the signal was still wailing, we would realize that something is wrong with the alarm.

Fear is like this. It is not meant to be a constant state of consciousness! It is meant to be in the background, on passive alert, ready when needed. But if it is sounding all the time, it has no value.

Fear feeds into our insecurities about attractiveness and has spawned a huge industry that panders to our concerns of being inadequate: "Without this product you won't get your man" and so forth. When you are susceptible to this kind of anxiety, you are vulnerable to exploitation by the fearmongers who bombard us 24/7 with reasons to be afraid. Fear sells. So take a stand against this kind of fear and those who would exploit you with it. Be an activist in your life; refuse to be manipulated by fear. See this type of fear for what it is: an unskillful use of the imagination that leads to undesired states of consciousness.

Only you can be the authority of your own energy field—you are the one who assesses if any of your mental activities are affecting your well-being for good or ill. You have to be able to read your own firsthand experiences. You know that these fear states are unhealthy, because you come back from these imaginary wanderings feeling unhealthy. Be your own authority, and pull your attention out of that which is unhealthy and invest it instead in something that leads to feeling vital.

To dispel the fear, use the four points we discussed earlier—the *map,* the *Observer,* *balance,* and *attention* (see pages 12–20). First engage your Observer to note if your fear is of something real or imagined. Know where you are on the map: unbalanced at the first level. Bring yourself back into balance with breathing, then use your attention to direct your life force toward something healthy.

Human consciousness is like a lake. In the center is the clearest water for swimming and enjoying, while near the edges and the bottom, it's not so good, kind of mucky. To get to the center of the lake takes some effort—you have to pass through the muck—but with a few swimming strokes, you are there. After your refreshing swim and you are back on the shore, you realize that tomorrow you will have to swim through the muck again to get to the clearest water. That is the nature of the lake.

At the sediment level of human consciousness we have the lowest and densest vibration: fear. Be aware that it is not *your* fear, it is *the* fear. Don't hang out in the muck and wallow in its yuckiness. Of course it's yucky: that is the nature of the sediment level of the lake and human consciousness. It takes a little effort to pull out of the muck of fear by using practices such as meditation, prayer, time in nature, reading sacred literature, lighting a candle for the suffering in the world, or taking a few conscious deep breaths. A variety of swimming strokes are available to get you to the clear water of consciousness.

I choose to dispel fear. I choose to feel safe and secure with life and myself.

Insurance or Assurance

Living with adequate health and life insurance needs to be balanced with living with adequate *assurance*—a certainty in the correctness of your path. Assurance in living your truth creates its own life-generating and attracting abilities. Your life becomes a testimony of the manifesting power of aligning with your most natural way of being.

EXERCISE FOR STAYING GROUNDED

The physical level is where you connect most directly with the earth and need to feel grounded in the here and now. When you are overanxious and have lost that groundedness, focus on the soles of your feet touching the surface beneath you. Focus on the base of your sitting bones touching your chair to feel grounded while sitting. When you need to feel grounded, imagine that you're sending your extra nervous energy into the earth, then drawing centered strength back up, as the great trees do through their roots.

THE EARTH

Earth: It is home for the species of humanity and all other forms of earthly life. In our time, global policies have tended to view Earth and its creatures as a resource for humanity to harvest as we please. The ecological crisis we now face stems from this lack of sacred awareness of our interconnectedness to the well-being of the planet. Without sacred awareness of the planet, we're in dire straits.

There's a legend that Chief Sealth (also known as Chief Seattle) gave this advice to the settlers who took over the land of his people:

> This we know. The Earth does not belong to man, man belongs to the Earth. This we know. All things are connected like the blood which unites one family. All things are connected. Whatever befalls the Earth befalls the sons of the Earth. Man did not weave the web of life, he is merely a strand in it. Whatever he does to the web, he does to himself.*

The knowledge was here. The awareness of the sacredness and interconnectedness of all life was here. Some of us saw it; some didn't. Chief Sealth's prophecy still holds.

Seven-Generation Thinking

We are told of many indigenous peoples who have a policy when making an important decision that will affect the tribe: they first consider the impact of this decision on the next seven generations. To those who treat the earth with sacred awareness, this makes perfect sense. But in our modern world, many would rarely consider the impact on the next seven years, let alone the next seven generations. Utilizing seven-generation thinking, we could be stewards of the planet and align with

---

*Although this text has been reprinted widely, it cannot be definitively attributed to Chief Sealth. Still, it articulates the wisdom of an indigenous sense of belonging to nature. "Teaching and Learning for a Sustainable Future," UNESCO website, www.unesco.org/education/tlsf/TLSF/theme_d/mod19/uncom19t04.htm, accessed September 4, 2008.

sustainable policies that ensure a bountiful Earth for future generations.

At the individual level, it can seem daunting: where do we begin to implement seven-generation thinking in our own lives? But we can start one person at a time, one step at a time, rather than waiting for global policies to change. You can do what you can today to adapt your lifestyle to an earth-friendly manner. Recycle, buy eco-friendly products, plant trees in your yard, bring cloth bags with you when shopping, be conscious of the chemicals you put down the drain, or on your land, knowing they will find their way back to collective water supply. Fortunately, there is a strong movement in this direction going on across the planet, and as it continues to grow we will learn more, teaching each other how to live sustainable lives.

ELEMENTAL INTELLIGENCE

Your body has been born out of nature and is sustained by your connection to the earth.

Getting out into nature or having some direct involvement in the activities that ensure your survival will enhance this relationship, such as chopping wood, carrying water, gardening, fishing for food your family will eat, baking bread . . . connecting to the life force that sustains you.

Earth and its creatures are alive with intelligence. The plant, animal, mineral, and water realms are the agents of that wisdom. Each can be learned from as a way of connecting to Earth's intelligence, and each must be listened to in its own way. A healthy attitude is somewhat playful and fanciful.

Rock, Stone, and Crystal Intelligence

The rock world is the silent memory keeper of Earth's stories. If you need to get grounded, hang out with a rock and see what it has to teach you. It's been around a long while and knows a great deal about maintaining essential identity through the winds of time.

Huge rocks are guardians and protectors of the spirit of the land. They weather all change, holding their energy in stillness. Any large rock that you place in your garden with sacred intention will maintain your objective with silent vigilance.

Crystals are formed by a molecular pattern that repeats itself over and over again, each crystal growing true to its pattern. The repetitive matrix creates a specific vibrational frequency, generating a silent tone. Those sensitive to crystals can use them as tuning forks to align with certain vibrations, much as one could with sound. With crystals the "vibe" is silent yet distinct.

Computers use crystal chips to record vast amounts of information—and you can use crystals as recording devices for your intention. For example, you can tell yourself that your quartz crystal means clarity to you, and you can hold and encode it with this intention. Then, anytime you need clarity, you can hold your quartz, meditate, and clarify your vision. If you believe this, it will work. Empowering the crystal with your intention activates your association to the call for clarity. Red and black crystals are grounding; rose quartz with its pink color heals a wounded heart. Blue crystals activate the mind and creative inspiration while violet and purple crystals are spiritually purifying.

Consider carrying a special grounding rock in your pocket to use as a touchstone when you are anxious and need to feel present in the here and now. Dark black or red crystals and gem stones such as hematite, obsidian, garnet, and jasper work well for this. You could also use a common rock from your own backyard or a beach or riverbank. There is a tradition that if you carry a rock from the earth of your home when you travel, you will safely return there, grounding you in your home.

Plant Intelligence

Plants are the lungs of Earth, breathing in carbon dioxide and breathing out oxygen in the process of photosynthesis. They hold the memory of the sentient world. Plants are the messengers that demonstrate how to adapt to the here-and-now conditions of your place on Earth. They feed us as crops, provide shelter, heal us as herbs, and nurture our souls as beauty.

Gardening as Stewardship of the Earth

Perhaps you have a window garden or a flowerpot as your piece of the earth, or perhaps you've been blessed with a yard, or even more. One way or another, become the gardener of your family of plants, and get to know them. Soon you may find that you can't walk by a drooping plant thirsty for water without responding; you can practically hear it yelling its needs. This is communicating with the plant—it expresses a need, and you confirm the communication by providing the water. Whether you have a single plant or a large garden, tending to the needs of your vegetable-kingdom family tunes you in to plant intelligence, empowering your connection to Earth and its inhabitants.

I've learned to use my garden as an editor. When I'm in my office I think up all sorts of ideas that might be suitable for workshops, lectures, and writing. My mind, however, is shameless and will think up all kinds of ideas, practical, impractical, or even totally unconnected to the here and now. How can I weed out the ones that won't work? I take my ideas out into the garden and tend to the plants and their needs. I've discovered that if I can't hold on to the idea while gardening, the idea is not going to connect with audiences. Conversely, if I'm able to sustain an idea while gardening, chances are it's well enough grounded in here-and-now reality that my audiences and clients will be able to relate to it and apply it in their lives.

Sacred Gardens

From the magnificent to the simple, a garden planted with the intention of creating sacred space will flourish with that intention and refresh all who gaze upon it.

Wildflowers are Earth's spontaneous gardens. Each plant has its own way of nurturing itself and offering what it has out into the world. This is the plant's medicine, its teaching, its vibration. Seek out these emissaries of Earth's sacred energy. They teach us how to adapt to the conditions of time and place. Spend time in communion with a wildflower and it will teach you something about yourself. How is the flower presenting itself? Hidden, veiled, or up-front and direct? Where does it thrive? In community, or by itself? On a grassy knoll in plain sight, or tucked into the shade of other plants?

Wild, untouched nature is rejuvenating for that which is most primal in you. Try leaving a space in your garden that is raw, let nature have its way and it will help rejuvenate the most natural in you.

Animal Intelligence

Relationships with the animal kingdom provide a direct path to connecting with the physical level. Nothing can cure feelings of isolation faster than the love of a pet. "I'm just trying to be the person my dog thinks I am": this bumper-sticker wisdom speaks to the unconditional love we can feel toward and from a pet. Although our pets can learn and respond to words, the true level of communication happens at a deeper, primal level. This animal intelligence stretches us past words as our mode of communication.

On Being Human in an Animal Body

Being in a physical body links us to the field of experience common to all humans: the drive for happiness and love, as well as our common difficult issues such as greed, lust, jealousy, anger, resentment, and so on. While in the human body, none of us can escape the human condition, and we all share in the joys and sorrows of that experience. The point is, don't judge your humanness. There are no saints here, just us humans, and each of us is vulnerable to the frailties and less-than-honorable aspects of humanness that plague our attempts to find fulfill-ment. When things are going badly, breathe it in and breathe it out and say to yourself, "This is what it is like to be human." Breathe it in and breathe it out. And when things are going well, again breathe it in and say to yourself, "This is what it is like to be human," and breathe it out.

Sports and all types of physical activities are key methods of engaging the physical level and keeping your body tuned up at the same time. Walking, hiking, and physically touch-ing the earth while you engage in a workout are ideal for drawing on this instinctual level of intelligence.

I WANT TO BE PEACEFUL, BUT WHAT ABOUT THE MICE?

Striving to live in harmony with the world around us, with-out creating harm, isn't always easy. I think of this when I weed the garden and decide which of the plants get to stay and which are discarded to the compost pile. I think of this when I have to deal with rodents, or even termite rot in my house, and I decide to evict nature's emissaries to reclaim my abode. When we clear land for a home and build a sweet cabin in the woods, we are claiming our right to be here. Life feeds on itself; we all feed on each other. Even the simple act of eating disrupts the flow of the carrot's or the cow's life. We would like to live in harmony with all of life, but then we disinfect our bathrooms so germs don't grow and we take antibiotics to fight off one life form to favor another. Where does it end, where does it begin? I want to be peaceful, but what about the mice?

I would honor all of the sacrifices of other forms of life that it takes for me to claim my earthly base of operations. I would try to stay conscious of all that I push out of the way so that I and my family and my plants can claim our right to be here. And I do claim my right to be here as an expression of my soul's needs in this life. Survival is the first level, and without it the rest doesn't matter all that much. So yes: survive and honor everyone else's need to survive as well.

Live simply so others may simply live.

———————————

When you are at ease at the physical level, it feels good to be alive. And alive is how you feel: vital, passionate, engaged with physical activities and some connection to Earth. You feel grounded, secure in your body and your place on the earth. Your senses are heightened and you are acutely aware of all sensations. This body. This earth. This here. This now. The physical level keeps you present. And when the first level is balanced, the energy naturally rises and expands to the second level.

TWO:
THE PLEASURE LEVEL
OF HAPPINESS

Chakra: Second—lower abdomen, just above the pubic bone.

Color: Orange.

Cores issues: The search for pleasure and the ability to enjoy life. Your personal tastes. Desire. Sexuality. Your magnetism. The seat of your personal emotions and your ability to feel.

Signs of imbalance: Excessive indulgences. Envy, jealousy, possessiveness. Treating others as objects for pleasure. Being out of touch with emotions and unable to simply feel. Insecurities over attractiveness.

Signs of balance: You have learned not only to survive, but to enjoy your experience of life. The sensory worlds of music, art, dancing, and romancing—all of these pleasures provide outlets for your celebratory nature. Balanced in your emotional body, you are comfortable with both outward expression and inward cultivation of your emotions.

When the energy of the physical level is balanced, the energy rises to the pleasure level and its many delights. Beauty, art, romance, and all the world's sensory pleasures become available, from music to food—what's not to like? Your second level of being awakens the desire for pleasure and gives you the ability to live a life of joy and magnetism. This level is the seat of your personal emotional responses to life's experiences.

THE DESIRE FOR PLEASURE

The pleasure that comes from healthy enjoyment of life is one of the great gifts of being alive. For those who know how to enjoy the beauty of our planet, there is still plenty available. Adding to your physical-level activities of surviving and thriving, you now incorporate the ability to enjoy the experience. You don't just want shelter, you want a home you can enjoy and feel comfortable in; you don't just want food to survive, you want food that brings you pleasure. You don't just want sex, you want romance. In short, you develop your taste. Your pleasure level awakens the urge for creative expression and the desire to live with beauty in the world. Dancing, music, and celebrating this life all come from awakening to this dimension.

Enjoy Your Way to a More Enjoyable Life

Those who have learned to master their pleasure level and the law of attraction that operates from this dimension have discovered how to enjoy their way to a more enjoyable life—entering into the experience of enjoyment when it is present.

Build your skill at recognizing these opportunities to enjoy life, and partake in every one.

Savoring a hug, witnessing a beautiful sunset, listening to exquisite music, tasting something delightful—these are all opportunities to expand on the experience of enjoyment. The pleasure of the moment is already available; you don't have to desire it, reach for it, or want more. Just linger in it now. Close your eyes for half a moment and enter into the appreciation of the experience, or even the appreciation of being able to appreciate. Not only do you lengthen the time of the pleasurable experience, thus squeezing out time in the day for less-than-delightful ones, you also increase your enjoyment exponentially through the law of attraction. The energetic message you send into the world is that you enjoy life, thus you will attract more experiences to take delight in. It is as if the universe is saying, "Oh, you are into enjoyment. Well, we have lots to enjoy—get a load of this." And all of a sudden the Universe Express pulls in, bringing more for you to enjoy. Remember that simple law: the more time you spend in a particular state of consciousness, the more you attract experiences from that state of consciousness to you.

Spend time enjoying today and you will attract a more enjoyable tomorrow.

EXERCISE: PLEASURE HUNT

Go on a pleasure hunt. How many places can you find enjoyment today? In the flower growing in the parking strip, the clouds sailing across the sky, an exquisite meal, music that liberates your heart? Look for these treasures and they are there for you to enjoy.

EXERCISE FOR CULTIVATING FULFILLMENT

Enter into the fulfillment of a satisfying moment. When feelings of fulfillment show up, learn to recognize and acknowledge them by saying, "I'm happy." Linger in the moment: the chase is over and the experience is on.

One opportunity for this is after making love. Spend several minutes focusing on your appreciation of the experience. Drop into your heart and be thankful. Notice how warm you feel and how every cell in your body seems revitalized. Be thankful for having a lover in your life who is willing to share the delights of lovemaking with you. Express your gratitude to your lover and hold each other while focusing on the deep appreciation for your shared experience. Realize that every cell in your body that is being born in this moment is encoded with the healing energy of this moment—love.

A warm bath with scented oil, candlelight, and favorite music is another opportunity to enter into the enjoyment of the moment. Ah! It doesn't get more sensual than this, unless you add some chocolate! Again, enter into the delight of realizing that every cell being born in your body in this moment is encoded with this deep satisfaction.

Living with Magnetism

As you increase the amount of enjoyment you bring into your life, your magnetism grows. Your life becomes enriched by all that you attract and are able to enjoy. If you are to live a life of great magnetism, you will attract all types of responses to your energy. Your light goes up, and others will be drawn to you. If you want to live a life of magnetism you must learn to deal with the consequences of living with a "spark." You will attract those who interpret your spark as special to your relationship with them and the confusion of magnetism ensues. You want to live joyfully—this is the pleasure channel—and yet when you let the full light of your magnetism into the world, you will get tested.

Let's imagine a simple, grade-school type of experiment. Let's imagine you have a magnet on a table with various objects that contain iron also on the table—some of them beautiful, some of them not. Now imagine increasing the strength of the magnet many times over and ask it only to attract the beautiful artifacts, not any of the rusty nails and worthless paper clips. This cannot be done; it is not the nature of magnetism. As you increase the amount of magnetic energy that you allow yourself to run, you will attract the beautiful, and the not-so-beautiful. In order to live with increased magnetism, you will need to learn how to deal with all that you attract. It is natural for others to misinterpret your magnetism. The hunger for love and warmth is huge and you will certainly attract those who are drawn to your light.

I think of the story David Chadwick tells in *Crooked Cucumber,* his biography of Shunryu Suzuki, the Zen monk who greatly popularized Zen in America. Suzuki was trained in the strict Zen monastery tradition in Japan and, at the age of fifty-five, was called by his higher voice to come to America and start teaching Zen.

Based in San Francisco in the early 1960s, he became a popular speaker. On one occasion, his assistant was driving him to lecture in a community an hour away, and on the way, she confessed that she thought she was falling in love with him. His answer was a life lesson for living with magnetism. The gist of his response was this: "Don't be worried about the love you feel; it is natural for you to love your teacher. Besides, I have enough discipline for both of us."

His answer acknowledges the attraction, but it also acknowledges the discipline required to resist the allurements that are always present for a person of magnetism. Learn how to deal with the ramifications in a healthy way. If another person misinterprets your magnetism, have enough discipline for both of you. But just as Suzuki did, learn how to sidestep the misinterpretation while still allowing the other person to maintain a sense of dignity.

Some forms of magnetism are delightfully innocent and always appropriate. People who work with the public need a touch of charisma; some people have a natural magnetism for animals. Teachers need to cultivate a healthy magnetism to keep students interested enough to learn. Playful fun between co-workers can add good energy to a workplace. Learning how to engage your magnetism in any activity adds a delightful and playful spark.

DIFFICULTIES WITH PLEASURE

And yet, many of us have habits and blockages that interfere with the experience of pleasure. Let's look at some of these.

Indulgences and Habits

Your pleasure level is your fun center—it gets you laughing amidst the dance of life. At best, this awakens you to the delight of your senses and, at worst, it may lead to excessive indulgences of all sorts. If pleasure is perceived as "out there" and not "in here," why not consume or acquire more and more of it? The balanced state of the awakened pleasure level leads to the experience of pleasure, rather than the chase for it.

I have had a lifelong lesson going on with this one, and it's become a family joke. I avoid eating much sugar, and for years I maintained impeccable discipline in that area—during the day. When chocolate cake was offered at a birthday party, I would dutifully decline. "I'm not into sugar," I would tell myself. I was beyond reproach in the daytime. But if that cake was in my family's refrigerator, invariably in the middle of the night I would sleepwalk to the kitchen and soon I'd be gorging on that cake! I mean gorging. Not just settling down to enjoy a slice—I would devour whatever was there, maybe even bringing it back to bed with me. If I woke up in the process, I'd be ashamed of my behavior. The family knew that if they wanted to have any cake, they would have to eat it before night, because it wasn't going to be there in the morning!

After getting caught enough times in the morning with chocolate all over my side of the bedding as telltale evidence of my night's adventures, I was forced to pay attention to the syndrome. It's as if as soon as my unconscious mind sees that my conscious mind is asleep, it sends the message to my body, "He's asleep—let's go get the cake!" And so it happens.

Over the years of working with this principle I'm learning how to consciously enjoy a piece of cake at the party with everyone else—how to enter into the pleasure of the moment rather than deny it. I'm still not so great at "a little bit goes a long way," but the principle works when you work the principle, and I'm getting better sleep on party days.

The lesson is clear: if the chocolate *is* the pleasure, then more is never enough. But if the chocolate simply triggers the pleasure and that's what we focus on, then savoring a little bit will be more satisfying than chasing after a huge amount. Spend more time in the enjoyment and less time in the search for it, and you are back to center.

To sustain balance at the second level, focus on the experience of pleasure, beauty, or delight within you. Savor the pleasure, don't hide from it, push it away, or look for it elsewhere. When you feel delight, be mindful of the experience within you and how good it feels. This is entering into the experience rather than chasing it, and it makes all the difference in the world. Quiet the tendency to grasp for more. Simply stop and fully appreciate the enjoyment. Sensed in this way, one mouthful of chocolate cake or one glass of wine does the trick.

The same goes for consumerism in general. If buying one item is good, isn't buying ten of them ten times better? Obviously not. We all know people who have all the resources and possessions one could imagine, and yet if they haven't cultivated the ability to enjoy what they have, they'll never be satisfied with more and more stuff.

To stay balanced with the awakened pleasure principle is to enter into the pleasure with awareness. Again, the rule is deceptively simple, even obvious: to balance the tendency to reach for more pleasure, simply enter into the pleasure that's in front of you. You are neither reaching for it (as if it weren't already there) nor denying it (as if it could be denied). Give up the chase and enter into the opportunities at hand; cultivate the pleasure principle as a skill, not a substance or experience. Learn to court the pleasure out of the little things right in front of you, like your interaction with the grocery store clerk. With an awakened emotional level, you know how to make the exchange enjoyable for both of you. Engage the world around you and bring a little fun energy to the exchange.

Recognize life's simple pleasures and then soak them up. Ask yourself, "Is my body working this morning? Is the coffee good? Is there something beautiful to see?" Then stay in the awakened enjoyment of the moment. Wallow in it if you like, but stay there. At the highest level you enter into appreciation from your heart level for the enjoyment you are experiencing at the pleasure level. This addition of gratitude brings balance and fulfillment to second-level experiences.

As you learn to focus on the actual pleasure rather than the search, your sensitivity sharpens and you need less and less to experience more and more pleasure. Certain indulgences will simply fall away as you engage in them more consciously and become aware that they don't truly lead you to the promised pleasure.

EXERCISE TO FREE YOURSELF FROM THE "MORE AND MORE" SYNDROME

To help liberate yourself from excessive indulgences, try adding a five-minute buffer zone. Instead of denying yourself the treat, go ahead and give in to your sweet tooth, but wait five minutes before reaching for more. Try not to feel guilty about your indulgence. Go ahead and fully enjoy it, then just sit with it for a few minutes to give the feelings of satiation a chance to emerge. This helps stop the gulping tendency to reach for more and more.

Unfortunately, this is not true if you become addicted to substances such as drugs, pain medications, or alcohol. With addictive substances, you will have to quit rather than wait for them to drop away—they won't. The addiction skews your chemistry, so you never get a chance to develop the subtleties of experiencing pleasure. When habits become addictions, you need more and more, not less and less—and you need help. You must return to a place where experiencing simple pleasure is possible. It is worth it.

Jealousy and Envy

If you deny or repress life's wonderful pleasures, you become vulnerable to envy, jealousy, or even bitterness. Jealousy and envy are both rooted in first-level fear of lack—the sense that "if others are getting what they want, there won't be enough for me, too." You might feel anxiety over your own ability to attract desired things to you. When you don't want others to get what they want, you send out an energy imprint of denial of pleasure. And guess what you attract back to you: denial of pleasure! Certainly not what you intended, but that's the way energy works.

The Hawaiian mystical tradition offers a prayer that is an antidote for jealousy and envy: *You can have whatever you want in life as long as you bless those who already have it.*

When another person has a quality or thing you would like to obtain, first, identify the natural envy that arises; it's human. Then try a little inner ritual to take its place. Redirect the energy towards your greater good by feeling the pleasure of knowing that what you want exists in the world and is available. Then envision those who possess what you want and send them your blessing. This pulls you out of the negative imagery and sends out the message that you take delight in people getting what they want in life, and that includes you as well as others.

YOUR EMOTIONAL BODY

The second level is the seat of your emotional body, your personal reactions to the full range of feelings that come with being human. Whereas your physical body is somewhat constant, changing slowly over time, your emotional body is in a continual state of flux and movement, like the ocean. The basic need of your emotional body is to feel. This is the emotional connection that starts with mother and child and reaches out to all of life. It ranges from joy to sorrow to everything in between, but its basic need is to feel.

Emotions might very well be the aspect of the human experience that we know the least about in our modern world. We may find it hard to picture emotions as a source for happiness when we live in a world that too often treats emotions as if they were a disease that should someday be cured! Even our language describing our emotional state betrays us: we describe ourselves as feeling good or bad, up or down, effectively judging half the cycle as undesirable.

We've become emotionally disempowered in our modern world. How long has the human species experienced grief, pain, loss, and disappointment? Millions of years, and yet we find ourselves at the start of the twenty-first century strangely unable to handle our moods and emotions. But we humans have, can, and will experience the full range of emotions, and our lives will be enriched by them.

Emotional Tides

For a healthy understanding of your emotions, consider their movement like the tides of the ocean: high tide and low tide following each other in rhythmic measure. One phase is no better than the other; each offers a balance to the other. Learning to think of your emotional cycles as "outward and inward" can help you align with this tidal part of your character. The words outward and inward carry less judgment than up and down. If you tell me you're feeling down, I want to fix things for you or help lift you up in some way. If you tell me you're feeling inward, I'll give you a little space.

You can create healthy, enriching, inward-turning activities such as spiritual practices, going for a walk, tuning in to nature, reading certain books, journal writing, or listening to music. All of these activities can put you in touch with your inner world in a way that is enriching and altogether better than just waiting for a mood to pass!

Quality Alone Time

Although your emotional body thrives on interaction, it also becomes frazzled from too much socializing. To restore your emotional body, you need some quality alone time on a regular basis. It's confusing enough to come into some acceptance of your own emotions, but with interaction, you end up processing other people's emotions as well and it can become overwhelming.

It typically unfolds that when you're feeling overwhelmed, you manifest some huge blowout or problem in your life, which so frustrates you that you have to get away by yourself to work it out. This is the reactive path—a kicking, dragging, screaming approach to your need for down time. The truth is that you may have needed to get away by yourself long ago. A more graceful approach is to set aside some quality alone time on a regular basis. Just knowing that you have retreat time available will give you more elasticity in dealing with the pressures of life. You know that a sanctuary is waiting for you.

People who are at home with their emotions feel comfortable in both phases of their emotional cycle, but in our culture quiet moods may be held suspect. Even in group settings, you might be very comfortable just being quiet within yourself, taking part by observing and absorbing the experience. But someone invariably asks, "You seem quiet, what's wrong?" Therein lies our cultural judgment: quiet = wrong. We don't like people being quiet . . . it makes us nervous. It takes courage to stand up for your right to honor your emotional body's need for quiet time, because there is no cultural support. You might want to answer, "I'm fine, just feeling quiet."

We lay emotional foundations with the language we use in speaking about our children's emotions. When a child is in a deep reflective place, we can imagine the familiar question being asked, "Is something wrong?" In our natural care for our children's well-being, we inadvertently give them the message that there's something wrong with inward-directed activity.

To encourage healthy emotions in others, give them space for quiet time and when you do inquire about their well-being, ask nonjudgmental questions. It is exploratory and nonjudgmental to ask, "How are you feeling?" "What's up, do you want to talk?" "Penny for your thoughts." These open-ended inquiries carry no judgment and facilitate open communication.

One of my sons was a bright, sunny, and popular teenager. His normal disposition was happy and outgoing. But about once a month I noticed that he was coming home with his head down and didn't want to talk. He would go into the TV room, wrap himself in a blanket, and zone out into TV land. When I asked him what was wrong, he would say, "Nothing, I just want to be left alone." He resisted my attempts to cheer him up and got cranky if I persisted. This cycle continued, and eventually I meditated on the issue to see if I could discover what was wrong. It came to me that nothing was wrong at all, just as he was affirming, other than my badgering him about his quiet, solemn mood!

I decided to change my strategy of dealing with this cyclic behavior. From then on, when he came home in this quiet place, I gave him a silent nod of acceptance and after he settled into his cocoon, I joined him on the couch in silence and watched the mindless shows with him as a way of supporting his behavior, rather than challenging it. We'd sit there for an hour or so and then the tide would turn. When his mood shifted, he would invariably jump up with his sunny self shining again and ask if I'd like to shoot some hoops or some such thing.

Crossing Circuits

One of the most ludicrous of all human behaviors is a rational argument over an emotional issue—crossing circuits. This happens to most of us because of our cultural bias: we don't recognize our emotions as an autonomous level of intelligence. We think everything should stack up neatly under intellect. But emotions don't play by the same rules.

Does resolution ever come from the following type of argument? One person expresses some feelings, and the other argues that these emotions don't make sense for such-and-such reasons.

If another person's emotional body perceives you as unreceptive and possibly a threat, it goes into defensive mode to block your energy. The emotional body defines your and anyone else's comfort zone, and if you are conscious of this in how you proceed with others, you have much better results. With consideration of another's emotional body, there is hope for progress. If you are not perceived as a threat, others' emotional defenses come down, and you're more likely to be clearly understood.

This can be most helpful when it comes to disciplining children. When children cross the line of some family rule, try quelling your spontaneous angry response and see if you can first emotionally connect with the child, understand the behavior, make sure they understand why the rule is there in the first place, and even take the time to explain how the rule is there to protect the child. After entering into the comfort zone of the child, then impose the appropriate discipline. Although they may still grumble about it, children disciplined this way feel comforted by knowing someone is watching out for them.

Soft in the Belly

A good test for knowing the state of your emotional body is to notice if you feel soft in the belly. If you do, your emotional body is relaxed. If you feel tight in the belly, your emotions are activated in their defensive mode. In martial arts training, this is desirable—you want to be ready for attack. However, in personal relationships when you speak from a place that is tight in the belly, others respond to the tightness in your expression. When you listen with a tight belly, you tend to perceive what others are saying as a possible threat. Speak and listen from a place of softness in the belly and you are more likely to feel—and be perceived as—compassionate, open, and understanding.

Breath is the best tool for regaining "soft in the belly." First feel the tension, then start slowly breathing deep into your belly. As you inhale, picture your breath dissolving the tension, as you exhale, picture the tension safely dissipating with the breath. Move into your Observer and suspend judgment, if only for this conversation. Feel the softness return to your belly.

To hear another person's emotions, it is essential to have a soft belly and suspend judgments. When you are soft in the belly, you are receptive and not perceived as threatening.

Emotional Communication

It takes emotional intelligence to understand the emotional body. Just as physical intelligence functions as instinct, and mental intelligence functions as ideas and logic, emotions require their own type of intelligence. Mostly they require a deep listening, but not to the words; listen from the heart and gut more than from the mind. If you are dealing with your own emotions, or those of another, realize that logic won't apply here, so drop out of your mind and into your heart and gut. Deep acceptance is required for emotional communication. Can you accept what the other person is feeling, right or wrong? Fault or no fault? That's what is required of you to emotionally listen to another.

If you know you are in an emotional space, realize that your rational attempts to describe it will be faulty at best. If you are absolutely mindful, you can let the other know you need to be understood at the emotional level, not the intellectual level. This makes all the difference in the world. If the other person thinks you're trying to be rational, your presentation will be full of holes and easily dismissed as "irrational." But if you can recognize that you're in an emotional space and need understanding, this disarms the defenses of others. You can say, "Look, this isn't about what makes sense, this is about my feelings." The other person now feels off the hook and will be more likely to offer the compassionate understanding you crave.

Keep It Moving

Emotions, like water, are most unhealthy when they stagnate—keep them moving is the advice here. When we attach to a particular emotional state and attempt to hold on to it, it always leads to disappointment: "Time and tide wait for no man," as the saying goes. Both with the emotions we crave, and those we avoid, it's best to keep them moving. Like waves in an ocean, or a ripple on a river, they are here for a moment, gone the next. Even painful emotions such as sadness and grief can be very healing if experienced when they arise, and then let go. It is when we attach ourselves either to positive or negative states that problems arise. The tyrant who will only allow positive thoughts to be spoken in his family is just as much out of balance as the individual attached to gloom and doom. To be in touch with your emotional body, you must be in touch with its fluidity. It is not as solid as the physical world appears to be, but it is just as real.

Cultivating a Strong Emotional Body

Cultivating a strong emotional body requires you to know what you need in order to be emotionally nurtured, and then provide that self-nurturing on a regular basis. No fair making your emotional well-being dependent on anyone else, either; that makes your happiness dependent on their behavior and not yours, never working out for the best. It would be better to take responsibility for your own emotional needs, make sure they are well cared for, and then share from the place of fullness. When you approach a relationship from a place of fullness you are perceived as someone who has something to offer, not take. It makes a big difference. Know what you need to feel safe, secure, and nurtured, and then set about providing it for yourself.

Cultivating emotional strength requires exercise, just as with your physical body. Learning how to cultivate kindness and compassion actually works. Pretend long enough and it functions like a jump-start, then becomes self-sustaining. When you're in the middle of working through an issue with someone, and you just don't get where they're coming from, try simply pretending that you fully understand them from their point of view, and see if that doesn't start the flow of compassion. We need to have compassion for others and their emotional experiences if we are to truly understand each other.

The Interconnectedness of the Emotional Field

Just as you are readily influenced by the invisible yet tangible sense of someone's emotions in your immediate environment, this invisible influence extends far beyond what the senses can verify. As we are genetically linked to the entire human species at the physical level, this is just as true emotionally. We all draw our individual emotional experience from the same collective ocean of human emotions. For each of us, our emotional body is an individual harbor on this same collective ocean. Each morning we can dutifully clean up our little bay and wonder how it gets polluted again, until we remember that the source is the ocean. We need to direct our attention to cleaning the ocean of collective emotions if we want our individual harbors clean. This we can do by helping others in need.

The risk of opening up to your emotional body is that you will feel the pain and suffering of others, and this is true. But if you can compassionately feel another's pain, touch it with mercy, bless it, and then release it, you have cleaned more than your harbor and are doing some good in the world.

Being an Emotional Laundromat

When your emotional sensitivity for others has got you down, try breathing deep into the emotion and picturing yourself pulling the feelings up into your heart. See the emotions being cleansed in your heart. On your out-breath, bless the emotions and send them back into the world. It's a bit like being an emotional laundromat—you breathe in all these soiled emotions from the world around you, cleanse them with your inner work, and send them out to the world all clean and ready for use.

It is a tremendous act of compassionate service to do this work of emotional cleansing, for yourself and others. It can seem daunting to breathe in the world's emotions, but it adds conscious, healing attention to that which is already happening. We can heal ourselves and each other, but not until we learn to feel each other. The collective emotional field of humanity is positively affected when you cleanse and bless the emotions that move through you, and this realization that you can help secures your second level of happiness.

———————————

Certainly one of the everyday miracles of our lives is our ability to feel emotions, and yet we've had to overcome a cultural bias towards controlling—more than understand-ing—this core human experience. And there is no getting around emotions; they come with the human experience we somehow signed up for. How skillful you are at swimming in these watery realms is a very individual matter. With the shift in awareness occurring from the reemergence of the Di-vine Feminine into our collective consciousness, emotions take on a new status: they are not only accepted, but also valued as a genuine means of communication. Perhaps emo-tional skills will one day be part of a healthy curriculum for living life. We're not there yet. So developing a strong emo-tional body in these times is a minor miracle in and of itself! You have to find your own way. The skilled are able to go to the tremendous depths of life with themselves and others, bless the energy, and let it move on. They allow themselves to feel the river, but not to hold on to it.

A balanced pleasure level activates the law of attraction, taking you beyond mere survival and into abundance and prosperity consciousness. You learn how to not just live life, but also to enjoy the experience. Becoming skillful in your emotions adds enrichment and depth to your physical level activities. When they are linked together, there is passion and enjoyment, courage and sensitivity, the ability to take action and the ability to enjoy the action.

As your emotions and the pleasure seeking of the second level become balanced, your energy naturally rises to the third level and you find yourself motivated to do, to accomplish, and to experience your power.

THREE:
THE POWER LEVEL
OF HAPPINESS

Chakra: Third—solar plexus, just above the navel.

Color: Yellow.

Core issues: Willpower, drive, ambition. Self-control. The principles you stand for. Your effectiveness at achieving your goals. Your ability to define your boundaries and initiate activity.

Signs of imbalance: Excessive competitiveness, or an inability to assert self. Tendency to resist anything. Control issues, power conflicts. Defensiveness when challenged.

Signs of balance: You have mastered the hardest test of all: self-control. You have learned how to stand up for yourself without infringing on others. You can define your boundaries without being insensitive. You are able to achieve your goals and are effective in all you do. You stand tall for what you believe in and are unthreatened by differing views. You understand there will be a learning curve in all new endeavors, and you learn as much from mistakes as from successes.

Your power level gets you standing up straight and gives you the feeling of wanting to make something of yourself. Its attributes are dignity, pride, willpower, determination, and self-control. Your power level allows you to rise to the occasion when more is asked of you than usual. It is the ability to follow through with a creative impulse, bringing it into tangible form. Happiness at the power level is experienced as satisfaction in a job well done or a goal accomplished.

The power level gives you the drive to succeed in life, to initiate projects, and to define your boundaries when needed. It can be seen as the inner warrior that defends your perceived best interests and champions those you love and protect above all else. Your power level gives you the self-control, self-restraint, and self-discipline necessary to pull out of the search for pleasure and make something of your life.

Activating this level gives you the ability to be effective in life—to say yes when you mean yes, and no when you mean no. Your power level is project-oriented: here you can accomplish something significant, and you define your character by standing up for what you believe in.

It is said that power corrupts, and there is plenty of evidence to support this assertion. But power doesn't necessarily corrupt; we've all seen plenty of examples of successful, authoritative people who wear their power with grace and dignity. Yes, there are problems associated with the use of power, and we will explore these issues later in this chapter, but first let's explore the healthy expression of power.

WILLPOWER AND SELF-CONTROL

We need willpower and self-control so that our activated pleasure principle doesn't lead to a life of hedonism, merely moving us from one pleasure to the next. An indulgent life becomes soft. Power awakens strength. It is the fire in the belly that says, "Enough focus on idle pleasure, I've got something I want to do." When you awaken your power of self-control, you can make some progress against the chaos of life. You can keep yourself on track with your goals.

Finding disciplines that are beneficial for you is the trick—not just the discipline of self-denial, but proactive disciplines that support a positive quality of life. You have to marshal yourself into getting in sync with behaviors that lead to your desired goals, or you simply won't achieve them.

The words "discipline" and "disciple" are closely related. At first, you have to discipline yourself to a healthy life until you become a disciple of your own path and the effort becomes self-sustaining. The first expression of discipline is often some form of self-denial: pushing yourself away from the dessert table, for example. But as the benefits of a healthy life become ingrained, discipline feels less like a stand against unhealthy choices and more like a stand for the qualities of a healthy life. The path itself becomes self-rewarding.

We are often motivated to self-discipline as a response to a particular problem, perhaps a self-defeating behavior we want to quit. How do we get a step ahead of the problem so we can exert our own power over it? Resisting self-discipline is all too human. We may need to remind ourselves: *If the whole point of facing the problem is to find the solution, why not move toward the solution directly?* We can get our life together kicking and screaming, or we can progress more gracefully. The will that we awaken to pull ourselves out of difficult times is the same will that can sustain our proactive successes throughout our life.

RIGHT USE OF POWER

With the awakening of this level, you get tested with the right use of power. Can you use your power in ways that benefit self and others? Can your successes be beneficial to humanity?

The Law of Power

According to this law: *Your power grows in proportion to how much you can accept and interact with all that life puts before you.* And the inverse: *Your power diminishes in proportion to all that you resist and pit yourself against. You split your power into its polarity.*

When you understand and practice this principle, you will see dramatic improvement in your personal life, your relationships, your work, your creative expression, and your spiritual life. Without this principle, will and power simply get in the way of happiness. You can learn to use your power in a nondivisive, noncompetitive way. You learn that it is to your personal advantage to work cooperatively with others rather than responding to the instinctually based desire for separateness or competitive victory.

The Authority of Power

To live in your power, it is essential to take 100 percent responsibility for the choices you've made and the consequences that have come from them. Are you self-defined or other-defined? Who gives you authority to live your life the way that you choose? Whose permission do you seek? Whose disapproval do you fear? If the answer to any of these questions is outside of self, you have given your power away. To walk in your power, claim 100 percent authority over your life and your choices.

If you haven't claimed the authority of your power, there is always a reason or a person blocking you from doing what you really want to do.

If You're Going to Do It, Choose to Do It

Walter Russell was one of the most remarkable men of the twentieth century, having achieved success in sculpting, writing, architecture, music, and advanced philosophical thought, to name only some of his areas of expertise. His sculpture "The Four Freedoms" is a national treasure. It was he who first used the term "New Age" back in 1943, when he announced the dawning of the next stage in the evolution of human consciousness. He believed that the level of consciousness that had been demonstrated by just a few spiritual masters throughout history was going to become more widespread.

When asked about the secret behind his wide-ranging successes, Russell said he had two. First, whenever anyone asked him to do something, and he agreed, he always did more than was expected, and more joyfully as well. Second, he only wanted to work with passion and his passion for an activity only lasted two hours at a time, so he needed multiple projects and fields of interest to pour his passion into.

The key to the first secret was that *if he agreed* to a request, then he would put heart and soul into the project. We can see that by agreeing, Russell consciously moved beyond the mindset of demand or expectation. Now it was his choice, and by claiming the authority of his choices, his power wasn't split by resisting anything.

The message is clear: if something is asked of you and you agree to the request, make it your choice and joyfully put everything you've got into the project. If you can't get behind the choice to this degree, maybe you should question whether it's something you really should agree to do.

I have a brother-in-law who is like a modern-day Walter Russell. He seemingly can do anything: he built his own house, built an airplane, designs computer security systems for airport fire alarms, learned the laws and represented people in his neighborhood in the environmental fight to restrict cell towers from wetlands, and is always there to help his family with his incredible array of skills. If he says he'll do something for you, he'll do it more joyfully and more thoroughly than ever expected. When I asked him his secret, he said, "I just figure if someone can do it, then I can do it."

Both of these men are examples of people who have claimed authority of their power. They assume nothing is in the way of stopping them from doing what they set out to achieve.

Effectiveness

Your power level is activity-oriented, and one measure of how balanced you are with your power is your effectiveness in life. Are you successful at accomplishing what you set out to do? With a balanced power level, you are able to accomplish your aims with determined focus. Of course the inverse is equally true: lack of effectiveness in life is a symptom of diminished power, suggesting a need for focus. Gain some self-control in your life somewhere, and you'll start seeing improvement in your effectiveness in the world. Start an exercise program, skip dessert every other day, stick to a regular sleeping schedule, hold your tongue, stop a negative thought—one way or another, demonstrate some self-control to get back on track and move forward in your life.

Mentor or Critic?

Does the voice of authority within you speak as the *mentor* or the *critic*? If it feels like a mentor within who assists you with your progress in life, the inner voice is helpful. If it's a brutalizing voice of self-criticism, that's another thing. Especially if it was difficult for you to gain approval as a child, it is now essential that you monitor your authority voice and gently change its tone and its message. Make it the voice of your inner mentor—a skilled coach who recognizes mistakes and communicates what can be learned from them.

Monitor Your Self-Talk

Are you being the mentor or the brutal critic with yourself? Pull your inner self-talk into line. Don't let it yammer away with belittling, disempowering prattle. It is your will that can help you move out of negative patterns and into healthy self-talk.

I was a young father; my first child was born while I was still in high school. I was thrown into the adult world of responsibility when most of my peers were in their high-powered years of social development. I became a schoolteacher, and with my students, my personality blossomed. I could be funny, engaging, and uninhibited around children. But with adults I felt all tied up inside. I was polite with them but expressed little of myself. I knew why I was successful with children: I respected them as big people in little bodies.

I was very aware of this split in my personality—at ease with children and inhibited around adults—when one day it dawned on me that perhaps I could transfer my successes with teaching children to adults, too. After all, adults were just little people in big bodies! I vowed to learn to be as at ease with adults as I was with children.

Even with this new awareness, I still lacked the actual personality skills of engaging adults in a free and easy manner; I still had a steep learning curve before me. In social situations with adults, I began to push myself to let my personality out of its bag. I began to take risks—although I often said the wrong or inappropriate thing and then felt terrible about it later. On days when the critic ruled, I chastised myself for being such a social klutz and I could feel my self-esteem shrink.

It was then that I became aware of the difference between criticizing and mentoring with myself. I was good at mentoring children—I would never think of belittling them for mistakes, and I easily donned the mentor role and encouraged them to learn from their experiences. Why not try the same thing with myself?

I kept my commitment to come out of the box socially. Each night I reviewed my day and noted my progress and stumbles toward that goal. As my own mentor, I taught myself never to take my awareness of today's mistakes into tomorrow. I would learn what I could from today's mistakes and start with a clean slate tomorrow. With this much more wholesome learning environment, I began to enjoy my efforts rather than feel tortured by them.

The Mistake Monster

Is your "mistake monster" larger than life? Does it paralyze you into avoiding trying anything you're not already good at? Are you deeply upset by the thought of making a mistake? If so, your effectiveness in life is being needlessly diminished. Mistakes are going to happen; they are part of the learning experience. Can you learn as much from your failures as you can from your successes? Train yourself to turn a failure into a learning situation, like an artist who notices what doesn't work in the creative process and adjusts accordingly. No one likes to make mistakes, of course. But you can get your mistake monster down to size by challenging yourself to learn from every situation. You will open up your field of life experiences.

Your Ego and the Principles You Stand For

Your ego creates your personal storyline. The pros and cons of having an ego might make a good spiritual debate, but everyone does have a personal storyline, driven by the ego. Your ego is what lets you know that you are you and not me! It is what answers to your name. Your ego has a healthy function; it's the voice that tells you where to go home tonight. Not any home: your home, your life, different from mine. This is the territory of your ego, your personal identity.

Having an ego is not the problem; we all have one. The question is this: is your ego aligned with that which is healthy for you or not? Your ego's job is to project and protect its storyline; your job is to make it an interesting story.

Hold on to your life's storyline and it defines you, let go of the story and it doesn't define you. Your ego will protect your chosen storyline—that's its job. But notice how the ego's protection of your boundaries doesn't allow for growth. If your ego wins at every encounter with life, you will always be what you have always been. So you have to be able to monitor this ego of yours: what is it actually projecting and protecting? For happiness at the third level, ideally your ego is aligned with that which supports your well-being, not just your success.

Skilled speakers and performers are excellent examples of personalities who can project a strong ego, yet can also step outside of that ego to cultivate a group mind environment. There has to be enough personality to make the material interesting, but not so much that the performer is cut off from the audience. Too little ego and the material is unanimated, boring. Too much ego and it becomes all about the performer, cut off from the group. Skilled speakers, performers, and group leaders watch this line closely.

It's helpful to have a sense of humor about yourself when you're engaging the ego and its territory. The ego will distort anything to suit its needs, and if you can see your own ego this way with a bit of humor, you take yourself less seriously—and you're halfway there. When your ego makes you defensive, you are in opposition to the moment. Learn to laugh at your resistance and see if compassion for yourself takes you the rest of the way toward moving beyond your ego and staying open in the moment.

This defensiveness often comes up with issues concerning pride. Pride is a two-edged sword—when you've done a good job with something and you feel pride in your accomplishment, this is healthy for the ego. But when pride gets in the way and won't let you entertain a point of view different from your own, then your ego is standing in the way of growth.

Your ego can't be eradicated or simply repressed, but it can be trained. This is your power level working on itself. You train your physical body with fitness work, you train your emotional body by stretching your comfort zone, and you train your power level by aligning with worthy goals and standing up for the principles you believe in. This is how you build character, and it's a key in the choices you make. Of all the principles and beliefs available in life, why have you chosen the particular ones that define your character? Some principles might be honorable, such as standing up for a noble cause, and others might simply define how you fight for your place in traffic.

I have a friend who demonstrates the honorable use of his warrior energy. He is a university professor who studies chimpanzee communication. He is also an avid animal rights activist and writes scathing reviews in scientific publications addressing research that mistreats animals. Other researchers are consequently very critical of him, but he is not fighting for his parking space—he is aligning his warrior energy for a cause he believes in. His willingness to fight for those who can't stand up for themselves has changed the way we understand our sibling species. He is making headway by advocating change in national and international laws regarding how chimpanzees in captivity are sheltered and cared for.

If you haven't claimed your power, your principles and beliefs will be born out of the "consensus reality," the popular culture of your time. The default question is "This is what I'm supposed to believe, right?" Without choosing, you simply become a product of your culture.

SUCCESS

Think of the qualities it takes to be successful: discernment, ambition, responsibility, commitment, adaptability, and a sense of honorable competition. These are the qualities of an awakened power level and will lead to success wherever they are applied.

Being a provider, achieving career ambitions, sustaining home and family, and enjoying relationships all require the same qualities for success, and what leads to success in one area can lead to success in another. Examine your life: Where do you already demonstrate these qualities? Where is it that your life is working, and you can't even imagine it any other way? The same qualities that make you naturally successful in this area of your life can be cultivated in other areas.

Tools for Success

Identify these qualities within yourself, then use them as tools. Aim them at something interesting: something you feel pride in doing, something worthy of you. Let's examine these tools for success.

Discernment

Your power level is where you protect yourself from all the energies that come to you—and it's also where you must discern which experiences you want to let in. If it doesn't get past the guardian of these gates, it doesn't get in. What you let into your personal experience and what you don't is determined by your discernment. This you gain by experience and observation. At your power level, your discernment is based on what is successful and what isn't—what makes your life work better and what doesn't. You notice the chuck holes you stepped in last time and you avoid them this time.

Your discernment also applies to your taste; it leads you away from what you don't enjoy and toward what you do enjoy. Being picky or being a person of good taste is only a matter of focus—use your discernment to focus more closely on what gives you enjoyment.

Ambition

Ambition is the desire to get ahead and get on with it. It fuels your goals, and if you haven't got big goals, start with small ones—but start. Ambition focuses your power and gives it something to aim at. Honorable ambition is aligning with goals that not only benefit you but spread benefit into your community. Blind ambition would be the inverse of the honorable use of power, where success is treasured at any cost.

Ambition is not just for career. It takes ambition to organize a community action committee, for example. It takes ambition to go on an adventurous hike or expedition, or an awesome vacation. Satisfaction is the name of the happiness that comes from completing goals along the way toward your ambitions.

Responsibility

Your power level loves to take on responsibility. It's not just wordplay—*responsibility* truly is the *ability to respond.* There are constant opportunities to step up to needs made apparent to us on a daily basis. Put yourself in situations where you have to rise up to perform. Whether it's responsibility to a relationship, a family, or a career position, your power rises to meet the existing need for it.

Once I worked with a couple who were in an unusual situation. They were newly wealthy, having done extremely well in the stock market a few years earlier. This allowed them to retire even though they were only in their early forties. They had traveled the world looking for their ideal spot, but since they could live anywhere, it was difficult to choose—they always thought something better might come along. At this point they had settled into our community not so much by choice but because they were tired of traveling.

They were in limbo—in the middle of where, they weren't sure; on their way to do what, they didn't know. Freedom sounded great at first, and of course it was until the idle time started dulling them to sleep. They were looking for guidance because there was no zest in their lives. It was easy to see that they weren't engaging their power levels at all. Since they didn't have to do anything, they weren't. This lack of engagement with their will and power left them feeling adrift, with no purpose and no community.

The advice was self-evident: "Get involved. Even if you're only here for a short while, get plugged in. Get a fitness program going and set goals for yourselves. Get involved in your land and create gardens. Take part in the community." And this they both did. He got involved with the county recycling program, using his business and organizational skills to get the program operating successfully. She joined the native plant organization that was dedicating its efforts to preserving native environments.

Their situation was unique in that they absolutely did not need to "power up" in their lives. Most of us are in situations that require us to stay on top of our game because life demands it of us. But still there might be times when you feel disconnected. When this is the case, engage your power source and get connected by finding something worthwhile to do and doing it.

Commitment

At the pleasure level, magnetism is the force to be reckoned with, but your power level responds to commitment. Commitment is there to carry you through to success when magnetism isn't. Magnetism is cyclic; it comes and goes. Commitment is constant; it just goes and goes. Success with power comes from determination that relentlessly holds on through the ups and downs of life until it has accomplished its task.

Relationships are an example. With commitment, we can endure tough times and come out the other side into joy and happiness again. It is commitment that carries a couple through the challenging years of raising children, surviving on scanty resources, and building careers, eventually to emerge to enjoy the bounty together.

However, our ultimate commitment must be to our well-being, and some relationships just prove to be unhealthy. In some relationships, commitment to well-being requires letting go of one another, blessing each other, and moving on.

Adaptability

Your power level gives you the ability to hold your ground, but you have to know when this is not in your best interest. Life happens outside of your plans; keep a keen eye out for changing circumstances that require a change in strategies. Don't be surprised by changes that affect your plans; expect them. Life is change; change is law. Simply said, those who can't adapt will not be successful, so it's important to weave adaptability into your strategies for success. The branch of the tree that is supple bends to the wind, while the rigid branch snaps. Species in nature are constantly adapting to their physical environment. Those who adapt survive.

Relying on your adaptability can lead you to adventures and wonderful experiences that you never could have planned for. Similarly, when you travel to new lands, it's great to set your itinerary aside for a while to allow for time to spontaneously adapt to the new culture and surroundings.

Honorable Competition

When your power level is operating exclusively on your behalf, it fuels the competitive spirit and the desire for personal victory. When your power is linked with the collective levels, it leads to honor, to success that benefits you and others, and comes at no one's expense. Honorable success is born out of community and is supported by its needs. In competition, honor is about respecting your opponents, wanting for them to rise to the heights of their ability—and for you to rise a little higher.

Are you an adversary or a visionary? If you live from an adversarial perspective, it seems that there is always something to overcome. Here are today's problems: how do I solve them? These are the challenges facing me: now, how do I overcome them? This problem/solution, challenge/conquest approach to life is the adversarial orientation that eventually wears you down.

On the other hand, the visionary gets up in the morning focusing on a view of what is possible, and moves towards manifesting that ideal. There are challenges and obstacles along the way for the visionary as well, but the motivation is entirely different.

Moving out of polarity thinking by rising above it gives you the ability to see both aspects of the polarity as part of the solution. This is synthesis thinking: being able to imagine a larger reality beyond right-versus-wrong, good-versus-bad, me-versus-you types of thinking.

I had a chance to see this principle in action as a Little League baseball coach for ten-to-twelve-year-old boys in a highly competitive community that supported a "let's win" attitude. Each team had twelve players, and league rules required that each boy play at least two innings per game. It was standard procedure for coaches to send the best players out for most innings and sneak the weakest ones in for the required two innings, where they could do the least harm.

But this sparked a battle within each team to establish the pecking order: who was going to play the most innings? It went without saying that the best players got the best playing time, and the rest got the rest. I was contemplating this during a practice early in the season when I noticed that the boys who weren't playing much would feel pretty good when someone ahead of them in the pecking order made a mistake. Their playing time depended on those mistakes, so it was in their best interest to see their teammates doing poorly! The "standard procedure" was holding kids down and creating a nonsupportive group mind for the team.

We held a team meeting and talked about it. I asked how many kids secretly felt good when someone else messed up.

Not everybody raised their hands, but many did, and we talked about creating a brand new team plan based on equal playing time for everyone. "We're a team and we're all in this together, so let's set it up in such a way that we'll all want each other to do our best." I was thrilled to see that even the top dogs took to the idea.

An interesting season unfolded. With our new system everybody was guaranteed at least four innings, and I could feel a much more cooperative attitude among the players. At first, the game scores weren't looking so good for our plan. But by midway through the season the tide had turned. With everybody getting so much playing time, all the boys improved, and eventually there wasn't a weak link in the lineup. By the end of the season we were on top of the league as a result of this cooperative team effort.

DIFFICULTIES WITH POWER

Difficulties with the power level run in two main directions: overexpression and underexpression. Let's explore both directions and consider some techniques for restoring balance.

Overexpression of Power

These difficulties range from excessive competitiveness to power conflicts to ruthless ambition, among other manifestations. What happens when we overexpress our power?

Power Conflicts

One sign of overexpressing your power is being excessively competitive, defensive, and reactive to anything that differs from how you want it to be. Excessive imbalance leads to a domineering, intimidating personality—the type who's winning at a game no one else is playing. Power conflicts erupt at the slightest provocation. You can be provoked by others who aren't getting with the plan and doing things the way you think they should be.

Learn to celebrate diversity. Be confident enough in who you are that you find others' views or ways to be interesting, or amusing, or at least allowable. *To have more peace, let go of your need to be right.* It's a simple slogan, but letting go is exactly the antidote for excessive defensive reactions. Practice the art of not winning everything, allow other people their victories, and then, when it is important to you, go ahead and win. But let there be some graciousness in your victories so that others can celebrate your successes with you.

The Adrenaline Junkie

It is easy to spot adrenaline junkies; they have the edge of justifiable anger. "I have a right to be mad," they say, and you are not going to be able to take that away from them. It's as if they won their anger as a prize at the fair! The ego justifies the experience. "I'm angry and this is why . . ." This imbalance feeds the adrenaline system and the body becomes on ready alert, too much so. Everything seen through this defensive posturing seems not right. This isn't right, those people are wrong, why aren't they doing what they're supposed to be doing?

Anytime you can get thrown off your sense of well-being by conditions outside of yourself, you are powerless, in a state of reaction to the world around you. When the source of your experience is external, you have given away your power. Performance-based measurement of your day is also an example of externally based happiness: I can be happy if I get a lot done today. I can be happy if my children behave themselves. I can be happy if my partner treats me well today. Here is an affirmation that can be helpful:

> *I do not need things to go right in order to be happy.*
> *I do not need people to behave themselves for me to love*
> *them.*
> *I am free.*

A story illustrates the idea.

In days gone by, teachers would travel from village to village, talking in the town squares to share their teachings. On one occasion, a teacher was beginning to share his stories when he attracted a belligerent crowd. They were taunting and jeering him and being downright rude. The teacher waited patiently and never lost his cool. After a while, someone in the taunting crowd noticed his countenance and spoke up.

"We obviously don't like you, and yet you keep telling your stories. Why aren't you reacting to us?"

The teacher responded, "What, because you are all acting foolishly, I should feel bad?"

This is learning how to not wait for conditions in the world to be right in order for you to be happy and centered. Do not be distracted by the flutter of the swords of discontent, which are always waving their menacing threat. You learn how to not give up your power to the conditions of the world. You claim your power when you stay centered, regardless of what is going on around you.

To stay in your power, stay in your center where you have options. When you're in a reactive and defensive mode, your perspective and options are dictated by outer events. You effectively give away your power by reacting to the situation at hand. When you stay in your center, you can witness the situation, create your own options, and then choose the most beneficial path of action.

Resistance

People are energy, and we interact with this energy all day. When you are exhausted from working with the public, what does this mean? It means you are defending against the energy, resisting it. This is a double whammy on your energy field. First you are expending your power to defend against energy. And second, you don't get to take part in the revitalizing energy that is coming at you all day through your interaction with people.

When it's resisted, energy that is meant to pass through you manifests as tension and has an adverse effect on your health and well-being. The person who can stay in nonre-sistance can run intense energy and sustain balance at the same time. Resistance tends to stop the flow of energy in the moment, which prevents the acceptance of the abundance of experiences that life offers. Why miss out? You can follow the periods of intense activity with periods of retreat.

Defensiveness

You know when your power level is in defensive reaction be-cause your gut will feel tight. Whenever you say something to a child, a lover, or a co-worker with a tight solar plexus, they will feel it as agitation. One of the things you can do for improving your effectiveness with the people in your life is to read your own solar plexus energy in the moment. If it is tight, know that the other person will experience this tight-ness as the main communication, no matter what is said. When you approach someone to deal with an issue and your solar plexus is tight, stop, breathe into your belly, and visual-ize the outcome you hope to achieve, then proceed.

You can also learn to read this in others. You can tell when there is tight energy coming at you and learn to step aside. Without giving up your power, you sidestep someone else's misuse of power; you don't engage it. You make the decision that this engagement is not a worthy use of your life force and step aside. Choose to not become a scratching post for others to sharpen their claws on. Life is short—be discriminating!

Underexpression of Power

At times we may feel powerless in life for some reason: we let ourselves be led along by the will of others; we feel exhausted by life; we fear failure; we have a victim mentality; we feel we have nothing to give. What happens when we underexpress our power?

The Service/Servant Dilemma

Being of service is something that feels good to most people. You want to be helpful, so you offer yourself in service. However, when the same activity goes too far, it starts feeling like you're a servant, and then it is no fun at all. You might ask, "When will they get it? When will they realize I've done enough today and need to have some rest? How much do they expect of me?" These are all the wrong questions. Try, "When will I get it? When will I realize I've done enough for today?"

Only you can decide how much is enough for you. Do you tend to feel guilty when you have to stand up for yourself? Realize "they" will never get it, they will never know when enough is enough for you. The world will gladly use another doormat, and if you are willing to be one, others will gladly walk all over you and not even say thank you—or perhaps not even be aware that you're feeling walked on.

Sometimes you can solve this service/servant dilemma by shifting your definition of yourself, as in the following story.

A client of mine was working with a particular frustration: She felt that her adult children were taking advantage of her, expecting her to take care of their children regularly—often without asking in advance, and just as often picking the children up later than they'd planned. We worked on shifting her definition of what was going on, and soon she was viewing the situation as a blessing: she was in a place in her life that allowed her to spend time with her grandchildren—and there was grace in it all. Later, the family moved and she had almost no time with her grandchildren. She reports that she is so thankful for having had the special time with them, rather than standing up for her boundaries.

Submissiveness

Many people have not awakened to their power and are just waiting to live their lives. "I was going to come to the event but my husband wouldn't understand." This attitude reflects a lack of power. Deferring to other people, being a good person, and not getting in trouble become a way of life. To people who have not claimed their power, the question "What would you do if it was your life to live?" doesn't seem like a joke question! If you haven't claimed your power, you will be led along by others. Your choices will be born out of the popular culture of your time, or a dominant person in your life.

It is often told that when people come to the end of their lives, they speak of, or quietly regret, the things they haven't done—not so much what they have done. Be bold.

If you are back on your heels with power and try to avoid confrontational issues at any cost, then you attract petty power issues like road rage, rude waiters, or other aggressive behavior directed at you. Or, if your energy statement to the universe is that others always pick on you, the universe will gladly oblige.

Often, people who haven't claimed their authority to make choices have relinquished their power to other people in their lives. When you feel intimidated by the possible repercussions of making a stand *against* someone's request of you, shift to making your stand *for* what you are choosing to do. Remember, your power diminishes when you are against something and grows when you are standing for what you believe in.

ACTIVITIES FOR RESTORING BALANCE TO POWER

In practical terms, how do we right ourselves when we either overexpress or underexpress our power?

Community of Higher Selves

The Hawaiian mystic tradition teaches of the "Community of Higher Selves." Each of us has a higher self whose job it is to assist you with any worthy goal or aspiration that you make. When the achieving of your aspirations will benefit others, all the higher selves of those who will benefit from your success enter into community with your higher self in helping you to achieve your aim.

When I was in my early thirties I was led to go back to college and pursue my master's degree in experimental metaphysics. It was a very busy time for my family. Laurie and I lived in a commune, owned a restaurant, and were raising four sons; I had a busy astrology practice and was a grader for the religious studies department at the university. Spirit was guiding me to pursue my degree, and yet I had very little time for actual studying. I became aware of the principle of the community of higher selves and believed my degree would allow me to better serve my clients. I put my trust in this principle and believed that if spirit was truly guiding me to get this degree, spirit would help me achieve this goal. I entered the program and studied between midnight and two a.m. every night, after first meditating on the community of higher selves. I was invariably led to study just the right material that I needed for the next day's tests and papers that were due, and finished my program with the assistance of spirit and the community of higher selves.

To engage the community of higher selves, imagine all of the people who will benefit from your success and picture their higher selves helping you to achieve your goals.

The Transmutation of Energy

Energy is energy, and for the person skilled at multilevel living, you develop skills for transmuting energy from one expression to another. Here's an exercise that can help. You use visualization and breath to transmute frustrated energy into positive fuel.

EXERCISE FOR TRANSMUTING FRUSTRATION

In a situation where you are hot and bothered by some justifiable anger or frustration, first reclaim your power by focusing on your direct experience of the energy of the moment, not the issue at hand. Pull your attention away from the event and toward the frustrated or angry energy itself. This reclaims your power. Now you are angry, frustrated, blocked, or whatever, but not because of anything; you are simply agitated. Visualize this agitation as a hot ball of seething dark energy low in your solar plexus, low in the abdomen. Next, visualize your heart and imagine it as a fiery ball of light, clean energy burning brightly. Now go back to the dark ball of energy low in your spine and breathe deep into it. On a slow in-breath, imagine that you are pulling the dark ball of energy up your spine with your breath. When you see the dark ball enter the fiery orb of your heart, see all the darkness and negativity burned away. What is left is clear radiant energy that you are free to express any way you choose.

It's the same energy it was before, but now liberated from its negative reactionary state, it is available for your free choice as to how to express it. If you practice this exercise, the process soon becomes automatic. You simply become aware that you are in a negative space and want to shift your energy and it immediately happens.

This negativity can be triggered by something as simple as reading the newspaper, watching the news on television, or hearing it on the radio. These are opportunities to transmute the negative news to energy that can be put to better use.

Entering Into Activity, Rather Than Doing It

Being tired at the end of a day is normal. But having your power completely drained is not, and it's a sure sign that you are making your life more difficult than it needs to be. Exhaustion comes when you are trying too hard. Essentially you are getting depleted from pouring all your energy into the day, and there is no energy exchange in return. Learn to enter into the activities of your day and take part in them as if there was an energy exchange, not just an output. When you enter into a relationship with the task, the energy to complete the task is within the vortex of the true need from which you are responding. You are still tired at the end of a day's work, but not weakened by the effort.

I'm often invited to various cities to do astrology sessions for clients. I call these "marathon weekends," where I often work with twenty or more clients in several days. Early in my career, these events used to wipe me out and I came home exhausted and drained. On one of these marathons I was working with a client who was dealing with the feelings of being overwhelmed by her busy life. I told her about one technique to forestall that feeling: stay in the moment, with one task in front of you. As I gave her this instruction I glanced over at my schedule and thought to myself, "Sixteen more sessions." And as I did this I could feel the weight of being overwhelmed drag my energy down. The effect was immediate and such a lesson for me.

The truth was there was only one person in front of me and we were talking about subjects I enjoyed. When I stayed with that awareness, the overwhelmed feelings disappeared. I learned that it is always this way. There is only the one thing in front of me that I am actually doing, and then there is the next one thing to do, and then the next. With this awareness, I still get tired after work, but after decent rest, my power returns.

Imagine the busiest day of your life and imagine that instead of all of that you were assigned to do on that day, you only had one item on your agenda. Would that be overwhelming? No. How about the next one thing you had to do? If that was all you had to do that day, would that be overwhelming? No. When you carry the whole day's agenda into every activity, you will feel the weight of your schedule, but when you learn to stay present with the one activity that you are actually doing, the feelings of being overwhelmed disappear.

Setting Your Intention

It's great to have goals, projects, or something that you would like to see come about—you've got the power; you might as well be using it with constructive design. Setting your intentions is a way of starting your day with your willpower aligned with your higher self.

Affirmations

Affirmations are a way to set your intentions by declaring the tone of the day in words. Some people like to turn their power over to a higher power, as in the affirmation "*Not by my will, but thy will."* This is not seen as a sacrifice, but as aligning with a greater power. Other people like to have more personal directions in their affirmations, such as this one: *"My life in every day and every way is becoming more abundant."* Or there may be specific things in your life that you would like to affirm, such as *"Today, I am enjoying bountiful health"* (or love, work, creativity, and so on).

Affirmations such as these consciously engage your power level and often produce amazing results.

When power is seen in its competitive guise, it often looks ugly. When we move out of a competitive model and into a cooperative model of living, power becomes our tool for being effective in your life, leading to success in whatever path we choose. Power starts off competitive when it is all about "me." Power turns cooperative when aimed at "we." Power becomes inspired when turned over to "thee." View your power as a tool to not only be successful, but also to create a beautiful life. Ultimately feel it as the Divine power working through you.

The power level is the last of the three personal dimensions that define you as separate from all others. When this is balanced, the energy rises, and interests of the heart call for attention.

FOUR:
THE HEART LEVEL
OF HAPPINESS

Chakra: Fourth (heart chakra)—center of the chest.

Colors: Green (some people resonate with pink for the heart chakra).

Core issues: The awakening of true care and love for others. Peace, serenity, and being at ease with yourself and life. Cooperation and win-win dealings with others. The seat of the three levels of love: personal, compassionate, and universal.

Signs of imbalance: Bleeding heart. Always being taken advantage of. Excessive worry for others. Falling in love with all the wrong people.

Signs of balance: Your heart is involved in all choices you make in life, and you've learned that love is the most powerful force in the world. You know how to draw on this fountain of love in all situations and always try to find a path that is in everyone's best interest. But most of all, you have learned how to love, and others are drawn to you for the peace they feel in your presence.

The heart level is happiness itself. When you reside in your heart, you see all of life through the eyes of love, and all your experiences are imbued with this sweetest of all nectars. Food tastes better, music sounds better, even the sky seems bluer when you are anchored in your heart! Health improves with the awakened heart. Your thymus gland, which secretes important hormones for your immune system, is activated at the heart level, so it is literally true: love heals.

THE MEETING PLACE

Your heart level is like an estuary where a river meets the ocean. Here, the individual stream of your life blends with the transcendent spiritual waters and in this coming together, love is found. This is the home of your soul—allegiant to and in love with your eternal spirit, and allegiant to and in love with your individual personal life. These are the tidal waters that come from the merging of the self and that which is beyond the self. The higher meets the lower; the collective meets the individual; the many meet the one, and the heart grows.

Awakening to your heart level allows you to embrace and celebrate the joy of existence with others, liberating you of all feelings of loneliness. As you pour your heart into life, all of life responds and seems to love you back. The heart is the middle path, the heaven-on-earth level. Here you are integrated and able to enjoy the delights of having a body, while simultaneously able to soar into the creative, spiritual levels.

The heart level is where you learn that love is the strongest force in the universe. Love heals. Love a person, a child, a dog, a cat, a tree, but love—that's why we are here. The more you love, the more you attract people and situations into your life to love. It is that simple.

To Awaken Your Heart, Smile

When you smile, a gentle warmth comes over you. Let your face break into a smile and feel this warmth. Draw the feelings of the smile throughout your entire body. Pull the energy into your chest and feel your heart, lungs, arms, and hands smiling. Next, draw the energy into your abdomen and smile from each of your organs: your liver, kidneys, spleen, stomach, and intestines. Smile from your reproductive organs, then pull the smile down into your legs and into your feet. Keep moving the energy of your smile throughout your body, sensing its parts as generally or specifically as you please. This is the feeling of your awakened heart.

When you meet another person from the place of the heart it is like the salute "Namaste," used in Eastern cultures as a greeting. It conveys the idea that "the place within me that knows God honors the place within you that knows God, and in this place we are one." The meeting place. When you meet another from here, you are acknowledged, the other is acknowledged, and from here no separation exists.

Love can be experienced at three different levels: personal, compassionate, and universal. We will explore each of these.

PERSONAL LOVE

When you think of another person and your heart warms, a smile comes over your face, and you feel a peaceful easy feeling, you are awake to personal love. Personal love is a warm glow that fills your aura with light. It is a desire for the other person's happiness even more than your own.

Heart love is unconditional love, like mother's love. It doesn't have to be earned and it won't get taken away. To keep the magic of unconditional love alive, never take another person, or any of your experiences together, for granted, ever.

Intimacy

To enter into the stages of happiness found with others, you first let go of referencing everything through the "me" focus. What happens when you are interacting with another and you stop focusing on your personal opinions, attitudes, feelings, and thoughts? The focus on "me" becomes engulfed in the awareness of "we." This is where intimacy is born, a merging of you and the other, something greater than just one plus one.

The heart level is where true intimacy is experienced. Without strategy or design, intimacy springs from the spontaneous merging with another. The deepest intimacy comes from dropping all the armor surrounding your heart. When you act in a way that is not aligned with your integrity, when you have some secret that you don't want your partner to know, an armor forms around that part of your being so that you won't get discovered, and intimacy is blocked. But when you are living within your integrity, you can be transparent with nothing to hide. There is no need for armor, and intimacy becomes possible.

EXERCISE FOR FACILITATING INTIMACY

Stay Five Minutes Longer

This exercise can facilitate taking down the armor and experiencing intimacy. Imagine the scenario: you're visiting a friend and giving each other updates on the news in your lives. What happens when you come to the awkward moment when you've both run out of things to say? There's a tendency to look at your watch, exclaim about the time, and get going on your way. Try something different. In this situation, practice staying five minutes longer. Not all day, not an hour, just five minutes. Stay in the awkward silence until something naturally arises, and what arises is born out of intimacy. Relax, and let your relaxation help your friend relax, too. Try not to fill the space with nervous chatter, just hang out in the silence and let whatever will happen simply happen. Now imagine what this technique might yield with a lover, a conversation with a child, a meditation. Try it!

Romantic and Beyond

Romance is naturally present at the start of a relationship. Both people instinctively know the courtship dance, and each tries to woo the other. It doesn't get any sweeter than the flush of new romance. Can it be sustained in a long-term relationship?

Certainly, but only with effort. The biological mating ritual takes over at the beginning of a relationship, and the magnetism is obvious. But how do we sustain that magnetism? Fun and games. They are part of new love, and they can be a part of mature love as well.

People who say they don't like games in relationships are going to miss out on sustained romance. It's all about the games! Of course none of us likes the game player who is out to get something. And romance at the personal levels can be manipulative. But when the heart is involved, romance is not about trying to get something, it is about giving and sharing in the experience.

Remember the games of seducing a smile, suggesting a special evening, or planning an unforgettable weekend? These simple touches bring a relationship up out of the ordinary and into the extraordinary. When you are bringing romance into your relationship and your partner's happiness is part of your agenda, you are in your heart.

When Laurie and I were first getting together, it was a very confusing time. We were teachers in a small school and were both involved in other relationships. Our attraction couldn't be stopped, and yet my mind couldn't see the way through the complexities of our situations. One day while I was contemplating the immensity of what was looming before me as a consequence of our coming together, an awareness came over me and I found myself saying, "Oh well, that which is born out of love will be lovely." And it has been for nearly thirty-five years now.

The Heart Breaks and Heals a Thousand Times

We are emerging from an era of emotional disempowerment when many have been taught, "Love is a risk—you might get hurt." We should know the truth: getting hurt is not a risk, it's a flat-out guarantee! If you love, you will get hurt in that love. Risk means maybe yes, maybe no, but have you ever met anybody who didn't go through hurt in love? And yet it is equally true that if you do not love, you will also experience hurt; the pain of loneliness and isolation behind the armor protecting you from hurt! There is no getting out of it: sometimes life hurts. But when we allow it, the heart breaks and heals and breaks and heals and breaks and heals, and that is what it does best. When you can go into the hurt, experience it, and touch it with kindness and compassion, you will come out the other side with more love and more empathy.

Loss, death, separation, and pain have been part of the human experience from the beginning. It is part of our species' intelligence to be able to handle these emotions. Trust this. Don't fall prey to the marketing notion that you shouldn't have to feel anything painful or even uncomfortable. Love and life itself sometimes hurts—so go into those places when they are the honest emotion of the moment and you will find the tenderness of mercy to buoy you up on the other side.

Insisting on a happy-face relationship by always ignoring difficulties feels superficial. This truth was brought home to me by a client of mine, a man who in all appearances was in a wonderful relationship. They had been together for twenty-five years and had two grown children. He was leaving her, and their separation stunned everyone because their relationship always seemed so harmonious. The issue that came up in our counseling might surprise many. He confessed that the crux of the problem for him was that he and his wife had never had a fight!

While those in highly contentious relationships might envy his "problem," to him this always being nice signified the lack of passion in their relationship. The message here is that having problems in a relationship is not a problem, but avoiding them can be. Going through a wounding experience with another and then healing that wound to love again adds tremendous depth and trust in a relationship. You learn not to fear the hurts or wounds, knowing that you heal. In the body, scar tissue is the strongest part of the skin and where a broken bone mends is its strongest point; your heart heals just the same way.

To know that there will be wounding times, but that you will heal and love again, is the security that comes from an awakened heart.

Deep Acceptance

Joy naturally arises through the practice of deep acceptance of the heart. At the heart level, competition gives way to cooperation. "Us and them" becomes just "us." You look for a way that is in everyone's best interest, and you love others as they are.

Practicing deep acceptance is a tonic that can cure most ills in your personal life. Relationships go through a profound transformation with this practice. Imagine accepting the people in your life just as they are with no thoughts of changing them in any way. It takes effort to change people, or even try to change them, but what effort does it take to accept things as they are? It takes the effort of residing in your heart. It takes letting go of the effort of using your will to shape, mold, and fix others. It is seeing and accepting others "as is."

This doesn't mean you won't want to help and offer advice to your partners, friends, and family, but by first practicing deep acceptance, you get to help from the inside, and the energy of your support and guidance is much more likely to be heard. Without the opening at the heart, your helping energy can be perceived as a threat from an outsider. Take the time to become an insider first, and then offer what you may.

Another client of mine was a single mother whose son was addicted to drugs. He was in high school and had gradually slipped from partying to using and then into abusing drugs. She knew something was off by his extreme and erratic behavior. One day she searched his room, found his stash, and confronted him with it. Upset, she began yelling at her son, threatening to throw him out unless he quit using drugs. He became defensive, yelling back that he was never understood. Then he ran away from home. Each time he returned they had another yelling match and the situation degenerated. With younger children at home and no partner to help her, my client was in a state of panic.

We talked about a strategy: connect at the heart first, softening the tension in her belly, and then communicate with more questions than threats. The next time her son came home she said nothing to him at first; she let him just be. She made his favorite dinner and they sat down and had a pleasant meal together. Then, with her most sincere effort to remove judgment from her voice, she asked how his life was going. She stayed in an interactive, interviewing mode and eventually he started opening up, confessing that he was addicted and very afraid because he didn't think he could quit.

She hugged him and still she offered no advice, nor threats. After they both had a good cry, they began to strategize together what options were available and started looking into treatment programs. They still had issues that would flare up, but theirs became a success story. He signed into a treatment center feeling that his mom was on his side as she learned to become his confidant.

Deep acceptance and the heart connection between them allowed for their healing to happen.

As you identify and learn to rise above your own defensive reactions, you can more clearly see these defense mechanisms at work in others. Knowing the futility of trying to get through to a person when defenses are up, you drop the useless attempts and realize that no ground can be gained with the issue at hand if you are perceived as a threat. Work on establishing trust between the two of you before you proceed with the issue.

Thinking from the Heart

As a child, I saw a Western movie with a scene that stuck in my mind for years. There were the inevitable battles between cowboys and Indians, with the eventual outcome—the Indians were forced to move on and make way for the onslaught of the white settlers. After the signing of a treaty, the military captain asked the Indian chief how he thought it would go for the white settlers. The chief responded, "Not good. The white man still thinks from his head."

Unsettled by the comment, I wondered, "Where else are you supposed to think from?" It became like a Zen koan for me and I continued to muse over it. With time and learning how to be in the heart, I've found that there is a voice arising from the heart—whether I listen to its guidance or not is another matter. You can court this voice by asking, Are the choices in front of me supported by my heart? Do they feel right? Can I get my heart into the choice? You can literally drop your attention from the brain area of your being and look at life from the heart level. Drop into your heart and feel.

One young man I worked with had a heart/head dilemma. He was on the fast track professionally and was moving up in the corporate world. He had been in a long-term relationship with a wonderful, heartful partner, but she had very little ambition. He didn't doubt his love for her, but was beginning to wonder if she was the right choice for his career. At the time, he was being courted by one of his co-workers who was equal to him in ambition, and although attracted to her, he didn't feel the heart connection. He was entertaining the idea of switching partners with his career in mind, imagining how he and his potential new partner could set the corporate world on fire together. They could host dinner parties for the bigwigs and help each other climb to the top of their field.

We talked about this head/heart dilemma he was in and explored what he was gaining from his heart partner. As he dropped into his heart and discussed his relationship with his current partner, he began to realize that she was bringing him a quality of life that he couldn't generate on his own. He began to see that she complemented his ambition, rather than reiterated it. He had plenty of ambition on his own and needed no help there. What he lacked and needed in a relationship was someone who could round him out with a rich personal life. His heart spoke for itself, and he had the wisdom to listen.

Listening from the Heart

When you listen to others from the personal levels—the physical, pleasure, and power levels—you are hearing from your own perspective, focusing on how the discussion is impacting you. When you listen from the heart, you experience the listening as a doorway to other people's experience; you hear what is being said from their perspective. This is empathy, the ability to literally feel what the other person is experiencing. The heart hears the words unspoken and responds to what is not said as much as to what is said. Others experience this empathy as a deep acceptance. They feel more than just heard, they feel understood and their illusion of isolation dissolves in your profound acceptance of their experience.

COMPASSIONATE LOVE

With compassionate love your heart moves beyond your own personal emotions; it actually merges with and feels the emotions of others. At first this might happen between two people who are already very close, but the compassionate heart keeps expanding and knows no limits. When compassion moves into sympathy, it moves out of the heart acceptance and enters into the emotion of pity, a silent emotional judgment of the plight of another. In pity, you are putting yourself above the situation and seeing it somehow as unworthy. Staying in your compassionate heart allows you to simply feel with openness and to share the felt sense of the moment.

Skillful Compassion

Many people fear opening up to compassion. They're afraid that if they let in the emotional pain of others, they won't be able to get out of it. But let's make a distinction here. Feeling another person's pain is one thing, but carrying it as your own is another. You don't want to add to the suffering in the world; that's not helpful for anybody. You can develop skills for compassionately feeling another person's emotions and then letting them move through you.

Second-level emotions—those in the pleasure realm—are personal. But at the heart level you open to collective emotions, so you may not know whether your feelings are prompted by a personal issue or you're tuning in to emotions that are outside of you. And at this level, it really doesn't matter. When you try to put a personal spin on an emotion whose source is really external, it can only create confusion. That's why the source essentially doesn't matter with compassionate love; the same process of healing is required whether you're feeling personal or collective emotions.

As a Boy Scout I remember learning that stagnant water isn't healthy for drinking: if it's not moving, it's not safe. The same is true for compassionate emotions of the heart. Feel them, bless them, and send them on their way.

EXERCISE FOR KEEPING COMPASSION FLOWING

Try this exercise: *Feel it, bless it, and lay it on the lap of the Divine.* Open your heart to the emotional pain and suffering of others, but don't carry it around. Let it flow through you like a mountain stream. From your Observer point of view, become aware of when collective emotions are becoming stagnant within you. Inhaling deeply, breathe in the emotions you are feeling. As you hold your breath, bless the energy. Then, on a deep exhalation, picture releasing the emotions and laying them on the lap of the Divine. After doing this deep work for several breaths, shift your attention and breathe in all the joy and love in the world. Feel the love, bless the love, and send it out to the world for others to experience.

I have been blessed with a positive attitude most of my life; I am pretty much wired this way. Rarely do I feel much despair or loneliness, so I definitely am aware of the periods when I do. One such period came at a time when I wouldn't have suspected such a deep hurt was coming. All outer circumstances in my life were seemingly perfect. We had just moved to the Olympic Peninsula to a house on a cliff overlooking the straits of Juan de Fuca. It was a happy time for our young family with our boys loving the beach, our marriage blossoming, all of us healthy, and my astrology practice thriving. Every morning I woke up in a bedroom perched like a glass-enclosed tree house revealing views of the sea life and its beauty. But I found myself waking up in a state of despair.

I reviewed all aspects of my life trying to track the source, and nothing fit. I could find no reason or familiar place to attach to this despair. Each day as I sat in meditation I would again ask the question, "What is the source of this suffering; why am I experiencing this?" My inner vision immediately revealed an image of a woman of dark skin with a sari wrapped around her shoulders and head, sitting on the sand and holding a baby dying of malnutrition, her eyes looking into mine with the burning question, "Why am I experiencing this?" Her image came to me day after day as I sat with this feeling, and I began to realize that it was not my suffering I was tuning in to, it was hers.

The feeling didn't go away, but I was lifted out of the despair with that realization. I found that as soon as I took part in any type of compassionate activity that day, like helping a client, making a donation, listening to my children, or even picking up litter on a walk to the store, it lifted me out of the dark. The source wasn't within my personal life; I was somehow tuning in to the suffering that is in the world. Directing my healing efforts to the needs of the world around me was tending to the source.

UNIVERSAL LOVE

The concept of universal love might sound a bit lofty, but it comes from humble beginnings: simply seeing things as they are without judgment while staying open to the heart of the experience. "Without judgment" is the tricky part! It's the mind with its constant analysis that gets in the way of the awakened heart. Mystics, saints, and poets have forever told us that love itself is coursing through the very veins of all existence.

Universal love doesn't simply come from a mental attitude—far from it. It takes an even deeper openness. Being open to this dimension, you experience all levels of love and emotion simultaneously, thus tuning to an empathetic alliance with all the agony and ecstasy of life, and loving it all. The wolf howling its deep desire at the moon; the poet searching for words to express a certain ecstasy—both reveal the voice of God in deep yearning. Longing hurts powerfully, but it is matched by the elation of desire being met.

This is the sweet agony of universal love extended into all of life. You see and feel the heart of the matter in front of you.

Attitude of Gratitude

To awaken to universal love, enter into the attitude of gratitude. Count your blessings. Think about what you feel thankful for in your life. This focuses your attention on your heart, and it always works. When you are cultivating gratitude, watch your defenses drop and your heart fill. Notice how easy it is to rise above petty issues and fill your heart with love and gratitude for the many precious gifts of life. This is a very real dimension of happiness that you have access to always.

GRATITUDE MEDITATION

Cultivate an ever-widening circle of love with this meditation. First imagine the person closest to you, and enter into the feelings of gratitude for the love connection you share. See the two of you encircled in love and appreciation. Then expand your circle by including another soul close to you who you are thankful for in your life. See the circle of gratitude expand to embrace the three of you. Keep adding to it by embracing another soul, then another, then another, in your ever-widening circle of love.

Laughter

Laughter from the heart springs from joy and compassion. Contrast this with the personal levels—the physical, pleasure, and power levels—where our humor often reflects a sense of separateness; we're probably laughing *at* someone or something. Laughter from the heart laughs *with* someone, or from a pure realization of joy and is born out of empathy and support.

Laugh often: it's great medicine for your heart and body.

Solution-Based Thinking

It usually takes some experience to grasp the absolute futility of the mindset that clings to right versus wrong, good guys versus bad guys. (It's just impossible to get the bad guys to agree that they are indeed the bad guys!) Eventually you learn to get out of the argument. At the heart level, the argument doesn't hold as much interest as the solution. You start moving to synthesis thinking, leading to a solution-based orientation to life. Conflicts begin to disappear as you have less and less interest in defending unimportant positions and more and more interest in residing in your heart.

Less Is Better

A side effect of awakening to the heart level is that you will be able to feel happy and satisfied with much less need or desire for input, outer stimulants, or sensations. A little goes a long way when you are open at the heart. Your skill at entering into the enjoyment of the moment gives you more and more satisfaction with less and less stimulus.

OVERCOMING
CHALLENGES OF THE HEART

At this level, as elsewhere, imbalances can result. How do we overcome the challenges of the heart level?

The Bleeding Heart

Perhaps the most common affliction of the heart comes from "all compassion; no boundaries." Tending compassionately to the problems of others without taking care of your own needs leads to the bleeding heart syndrome. You seem to invite other people to take advantage of you. This tendency is born out of a huge heart; you feel so sorry about others' plights that you want to do everything you can do to help them. What could be wrong with this? Plenty. If you don't take care of your own boundaries and honor what's in your own best interest, you set yourself up for these boundaries being crossed, and the sense of violation that ensues.

You need to learn to include yourself in your heart circle of the people you most care about. Do the caring thing for yourself, just as you would for another. You have to include your own best interests in all that you agree to do. Whatever it is, it never works out if it is about sacrifice.

The tendency of the bleeding heart is to give until it hurts, which it eventually does. The high road always has to lead to your best interest *and* the other person's best interest as well. A balanced exchange can never come from sacrifice. You have to know when enough is enough, when to pull back and take care of your own business. Only then will you be able to successfully contribute to the lives of others in a heartful way.

Falling in Love with All the Wrong People

When you open to your heart, it's natural to feel love for almost everything and everybody. It's a beautiful thing to see another's shining potential, and at the spiritual level, this could never be wrong. The challenge comes when you try to make this into personal love. You see a person struggling at the personal levels, but you rise above the issues and connect at the heart. Love happens. When you fall in love with another's potential, but not the present-day actuality of that person, disappointment always follows.

Before you get deeply involved with another, ask yourself this critical question: "If this person does not change one little bit, would I still be attracted?" This doesn't mean that a person must be perfect. There may be some traits that are not desirable to you but you know you can handle them, and some that you absolutely cannot. Of course we want to allow room for growth in another, but if you have a tendency to fall in love with all the wrong people, pull back and honestly ask yourself: Am I falling in love with the potential, or the actual?

Needing to Be Needed

Your compassionate heart feels best when needed. You love to help. When you find another person who has difficulties, it almost feels good, because you know you're going to be needed and appreciated. All of this is fine so far. But if this is the basis of your energy exchange—your partner needs help, you need to help—it may seem to be a perfect arrangement at first, yet it's not so perfect if it becomes the constant. If this is the energy agreement between the two of you—one gives, the other receives—it fits the definition of a codependent relationship. In a strange way, this arrangement actually tends to hold people in their problems: that's where they're getting the love.

If the dynamic is issue-based or time-based, it's probably not a problem. If you're helping another with a specific difficulty or a specific tough time, this energy arrangement is healthy and honorable. It becomes unsatisfactory when it becomes the 24/7 of the relationship.

The antidote is to give others silent support and strength, believing in your heart that they can rise above their own issues. In the end, we can help others, but ultimately they need to be able to face and deal with their own issues, or the help doesn't take. When you do the work for others, when your will sustains their work, it might give them a jump start, but unless they invest their own will in the helping direction, the growth isn't sustainable. Know that *not* helping can be an act of compassion at times. You pull back, offer silent support, and give others the opportunity to make a growth step on their own. If you're doing the work for them, they don't get to keep it anyway.

Some time ago a young couple came to my practice, a pair with huge hearts and huge money and whose extended family had huge problems. They had fallen into a pattern of rescuing their family by financially bailing them out of their constant economic woes. A pattern was set that over time led to a financial burden of massive debt. The energy exchange of "give til it hurts" was hurting.

Their mind-set was based in a generous and beautiful question: "What do you do when someone you love has needs?" Their default answer was that you give and do everything possible to help. The heart behind their motivation was strong, but they were undermining the balanced exchange we all need with life: to give and receive. If you've made a depletion energy-exchange agreement with the world, whether it is emotional or financial, depletion will be the result and the measure of this exchange.

To this couple, not giving to others seemed like tough love rather than compassion. But they eventually understood that to believe in others is to believe that they have within them all that they need to succeed. They brought their overgiving under control and got out of debt.

Sometimes it's the panic of a dire situation that activates the inner strength to deal with it. Imagine a chick growing inside an egg. At a certain point, the panic of the confinement overwhelms the comfort of the protective shell, and the chick breaks through it to enter into a whole new stage of growth and development. As it does so, it exercises its own life force. Helping the chick out of the egg robs it of its own strength.

It's an act of compassion to pull back when your help is enabling another to stay in a codependent state. Step back and let the person develop the strength to deal with the issue at hand.

Overcoming Depletion

Those awakening to the heart level may go through periodic spells of depletion. The heart level invokes generosity, and this is good as long as it is not a depletion model. If your energy statement is "I'm more comfortable giving than receiving," it's a depletion model. Can you imagine speaking this affirmation? "At the end of the day, I want to feel that I have less than I started with." Of course you wouldn't want to tell yourself that, but those who are more comfortable giving than receiving are saying exactly that in their energetic arrangement with life. Imagine a bank with a policy of lending more money than it received. Imagine a well that pumped out more water than it could replenish. How is this going to work out over time? A depletion model leads to exhaustion.

Imagine that a neighbor comes over to your house and asks for assistance with a project. You gladly help out, and the next day your neighbor comes over again, this time with soap and bucket in hand. He wants to wash your car as thanks for helping him out last night. In our scenario, let's imagine that you say, "Oh don't bother, it's not necessary." So how does your neighbor feel when he leaves? Rejected? Denied? Energetically, you're telling him that you don't value what he has to offer—that you helped out last night, but let's not make this a regular thing. As time goes by, you start noticing that your neighbor never asks you for help anymore, and you wonder what you did to offend him.

Those who are more comfortable giving than receiving have a fire hose going from their hearts and a straw coming back in. With this image, the work isn't to shrink the fire hose, but to expand the straw. Learn to be gracious in receiving compliments, help, and returned favors. Notice your tendency to decline, and then open up the straw and receive and appreciate the energy coming to you. This will help restore balance to your giving and receiving of energy so that you begin to receive as much from the universe as you put out into it.

"Joyfully I give, and joyfully I receive" is a wonderful mantra for restoring balance.

Overcoming Burnout

You've awakened to the heart and you're giving, giving, giving, but you've forsaken the source. If the "I," the ego, is doing the giving, you will soon be spent and exhausted. If you have the sense that "I gave everything I had" or "I'm doing so much for others," take a look—it may be about your ego.

If you can tap into the source, you draw the universal energy through you. You're giving, but at the same time you're receiving. Give from the heart as long as it feels good—not until it hurts. This is your barometer; take responsibility for maintaining your own energy, not letting it get run down.

It's better to give 100 percent 50 percent of the time than to give 50 percent 100 percent of the time. If you're giving, giving, giving, all the time, there's no way you can give your best. Realize that it's better to monitor yourself so that you stay at your best. Then, when you are helping others, your joy in giving comes with it.

Overcoming Worry

Concern for others is a natural outpouring of the awakened heart. But when compassion drifts into worrying, you are inadvertently sending those you love negative energy. What is worry? Worry is negative prayer. It's wrapping another in your fears and calling it love. It is wise to be responsible with our energy exchange with the people we love and avoid sending negative thoughts about what might go wrong. Instead, we can learn to send empowering thoughts, white light, or protective angels.

EXERCISE FOR TRANSFORMING WORRY

This mental exercise helps me when I drift into worry for those I love. I try to imagine an artist capturing my worry in a painting. My heavy, dark emotions would be captured in the muddled colors and dense shapes on the canvas. Then I imagine having the painting framed and gift-wrapped and giving it to the person I'm worrying about, saying, "When you want to know what kind of energy I'm sending you, look at this painting and you'll feel my energy." This image helps me to realize that it wouldn't be a gift at all! With this sharp reminder, I can then create a painting that is more worthy of the energy I would really like to send—energy to help, love, and lift.

Expanding the Territory of Your Vows

Have you taken vows to deny self in favor of God, either in this life or in previous lives? If so, the vows may serve as a painful reminder of feeling bad when you feel good about yourself. Try expanding your dedication to the Divine—expand on your vows to see the Divine in all of creation. You can't go back on a vow without all types of backlash, but you can expand on your commitment to God. Try expanding your love of the Divine so that you can also behold our planet's great gifts of sensory delights bestowed on us. Vows of denial limit the terms on which you can meet the Divine. Expand the territory to love the Divine in all of its manifestations, including yourself and your worldly nature while you are in a body. Experience the love of creation through the delight of your senses. Let God and Goddess love creation through you.

The heart is where we feel the heaven-on-earth that our life here can be when it all comes together. When you're able to reside at the heart level, you've learned that love is the strongest force in the world, and your experience of life changes dramatically with this awakening. You see evidence of kindness and compassion everywhere. Others are drawn to you because of the peace they feel in your presence. You've let go of the struggles of existence that plague the lower levels, and although you still have your challenges, you meet them with equanimity and grace. You've learned to tap into the inexhaustible source of Divine love, and when you give to others from this place, you feel that love moving through you. You know that in the end, what counts is the love you experience and share with others. Love is.

To quote Bobby, "It's all about the love, man."

FIVE:
THE EXPRESSION LEVEL
OF HAPPINESS

Chakra: Fifth—the throat.

Color: Sky blue.

Core issues: The need to express yourself and to be authentic in what you say and do. Creative expression. Insights, intuition, and access to the universal mind. Invention and innovation. Truth. Originality.

Signs of imbalance: Inappropriate expression of self— either too little or not enough. Disruptive tendencies, always fighting for the right to be free. Anxiety.

Signs of balance: Others rely on you to speak your truth, and you do. You have put together your own unique worldview, and act on it without needing to prove yourself to others. You can be counted on to offer originality and fresh insights. You have learned how to quiet your thinking mind so that you may listen to the subtle guidance of intuition.

The happiness that comes from gaining the freedom of self-expression is the ability to speak your truth. At this level, you are free from needing support and approval for your path and have gained the mastery of self-expression. The expression level not only liberates you to express yourself, it also awakens your intuition, the wonderful gift of insight that gives you access to information you didn't even know you had. Writers, artists, actors, and free thinkers of all sorts draw heavily from this level. From this level, you offer originality in all that you do, whether in the arts, business, relationships, or in personal pursuits. You become more of an inventor than a follower. This is where you speak your truth and demand that others speak their truth as well.

Freedom of expression depends upon freedom of thinking. You have to know your truth to speak your truth. Therefore all matters connected to your mental and intuitive processes come into play: How free are you to express yourself? What is it that you know, and how can you share this with the world?

FREEDOM FROM CULTURAL CONDITIONING

During your childhood years you received a tremendous amount of cultural conditioning, for good or for ill. These are the years when children learn from their culture what to expect in life. In your first few years this conditioning was the preconscious imprinting you received in the home you were born into. In the school years you received conditioning through your schoolmates and the teachers. Families, friends, churches, schools, television, music, the Internet, and the news are all part of the cultural web of influence that has formed many of your beliefs and expectations. And so we learn, and so it goes.

With the first stirrings of yearning for freedom of expression you begin to question this view of the "world according to others." You begin to suspect that your opinions and views might be just as valid as anyone else's. At this stage, "because it's always been done that way" is no longer reason enough to follow conventional rules, or even to follow peoples whose path differs from yours. You may question authority, question rules, question the status quo in all ways; you may even question other people's views if they don't demonstrate original thinking. If they're just passing on what they heard elsewhere, you are not interested. If they've given it some thought and are offering original insights, you are all ears.

Perhaps we would all like to believe that if we had been around in the time of slavery in the American South, or witnessed any other barbaric practice, we would have stood up and questioned what was going on. It would have taken the same strength of character then that it takes now to break out of culturally induced sleepwalking and wake up to discover our own personal values. It takes courage to question authority when it doesn't resonate with our truth.

The first step of awakening to the freedom of expressing yourself is to be willing to question everything you have been taught, to stack it up against how you see things. Do you have the character strength to go with your own view when it differs from the cultural norm? This is what it takes to have an awakened and sustained expression level of consciousness. This is the path towards authenticity and originality. You have to be willing to break free of the pack. But it's not just breaking free as in rebelling against convention—it's the freedom of finding your own authentic truth.

You might travel the world and sample it all, then return home to your roots, taking up the family land or business. Or you might explore through books, people, and life experiences and choose a very different path from the one you saw in your family of origin. The point is to come home to your genuine truth after an authentic search—whether or not that genuine truth fits with your upbringing.

AUTHENTICITY

The true hunger of this level is to be authentic. You can seem rebellious or eccentric to others when you don't conform to their expectations, but authenticity comes from not needing anyone outside of yourself to verify your truth. You know what you know from your own life experience, and you will not be dissuaded from your truth. The benefit here is obvious: you don't have to convince anyone. You don't have to gain permission for your truth.

If you are going to be authentic, the culture often labels you eccentric. Expect it. Every great artist, inventor, and original thinker who received this voice and acted on it has been considered eccentric by society. It's a requirement for greatness. That's why it takes such confidence to listen to your authentic voice; by definition, there won't be cultural support for it. This is where you must have absolute authority in interpreting your truth.

If you back down from your truth to conform to cultural expectations, you forsake your authentic insights and settle for the elastic pull of those expectations. It takes absolute freedom from consensus reality to listen to and directly perceive your truth. Your truth may fit with cultural standards or not; that is not the point. The point is that your truth is not born out of your cultural training—it is your direct, unfiltered way of perceiving.

Your Right to Be Free: Fighting for It and Expressing It

As you first awaken to this stage of knowing your individual truth, you might feel edgy and rebellious. Maybe you seem to attract people and situations that attempt to control or limit you. You will have none of that! You will actively engage the battle to overthrow the restricting force, proving that no one can control you.

As you stay with this, you eventually tire of constantly having to prove your freedom over and over again. You eventually get the cosmic joke: if you need someone else's approval to be free, you are not all that free in the first place! At this point, you get on to expressing your right to be free. You no longer attract those controlling voices, or at least you no longer engage them. When you are free of having to prove yourself, there is nothing within you that needs defending. You have true freedom to express your innovative ideas without hesitation. Removing yourself from needless resistance conserves your energy for more interesting topics and creative outlets.

You become an independent thinker, free from having to conform to anyone's view of how you should live your life. Freedom doesn't need anything; it's free. It doesn't need the support of churches, books, or teachers. You are willing to stand on the truth of your own perceptions.

Get Out of the Way and Let the Creativity
Be Expressed Through You

How do you get yourself out of the way and allow the collective mind to express through you? It comes from hooking up, from being open to the sea of creative ideas that are floating around waiting for someone to host the creative act. Get the "I" from your personal levels out of the way and let yourself access the collective intelligence that is part of your heritage.

When you say, "I don't know if I can be that creative," have a laugh at yourself for assuming that your personal "I" is going to do it anyway! Then allow the universal creative energy to express through you.

It is utterly amazing what we can do collectively. I recently watched for a while as the Tacoma Narrows Bridge was being built. It's a suspension bridge over a mile long with a drop of almost two hundred feet to the water below. No one individual could make that happen; the power of our collective abilities united toward worthy goals is awe-inspiring. I recently learned of an Internet-accessed database where doctors the world over can share their experiences with various procedures and medications. Now, healers around the world can directly learn from each other in this new venue, one that may have some advantages over the published research that is often sponsored. This shared knowledge may greatly accelerate the learning curve as to what works and what doesn't in medical developments.

The rise of the euro is another example of this power. With the creation of a common currency that transcends national differences in Europe, a fluid movement of commerce and ideas between all the participating countries has occurred, and the euro has risen as one of the strongest currencies in the world.

The author Paul Hawken, in *Blessed Unrest*, describes what he calls the largest movement in the history of humanity, one that has largely gone unreported.* He cites evidence of a global network of thousands of organizations involving millions of people in the environmental and cooperative food movements who are sharing information and resources without any central leadership. It is evolving out of common needs and interests without any organization directing it.

Write Your "Morning Pages"

In creative circles inspired by Julia Cameron's book *The Artist's Way*, many people follow the practice of writing three pages nonstop every morning. They may write the same word over and over again for a while, if they must, but they

---

*Paul Hawken, *Blessed Unrest* (New York: Penguin, 2008).

don't stop writing. This tradition of "morning pages" provides a good way to empty out the "me" stuff, clearing space for inspired material to come in. It's best to do it first thing in the morning, before the day gets hold of you. Write in a stream-of-consciousness style without planning, punctuating, or even holding on to a thought. Just be a scribe to the ever-changing panorama in your mind. Typically, the first few pages empty the "me" material; in later pages, juicier, inspired flashes of insight are more likely.

It's helpful to know that no one will ever read these pages; use them only for this exercise, then recycle them. Ceremonial burning is another way of cutting loose of the material. You needn't even write in a journal; an informal spiral-bound notebook works best. Let your handwriting style reflect this mad dash to empty yourself—no need for carefully formed letters.

Higher-Level Energy Surges: Inspiration or Anxiety?

Insights, flashes of awareness, and sudden knowing all come from tuning in to the collective mind—but what else is likely to come along with these downloads from the mainframe computer in the sky? Energy. Huge energy surges. If not understood, these surges can be felt as anxiety attacks, nervousness, and feelings of uncertainty. When this is the case, the energy download is happening, but the energy is thought to be problematic and is therefore resisted. Anxiety, nervousness, and uncertainty are felt when these surges are resisted.

These surges are too much energy for the personal levels to handle by themselves. When you're locked into the lower levels and yet experiencing energy surges from your upper levels, there's too much energy for too little space and you feel that you may explode. Breathe. Literally breathe more deeply, more slowly, and your ability to be with the energy improves dramatically. The energy doesn't actually subside, but you create more space for that energy, so the feeling of compression dissipates.

Now, using your breath, you are riding the wave instead of attempting to quiet the wave, and you enter into a state of heightened awareness. Grab a pencil and a notebook because ideas come flooding in while you are with the energy. Don't assume these ideas will stick around. Sketch them, write them, but don't let these become whistles on the wind.

As strange as it sounds, you may be accessing information outside of the current space-time continuum. Don't assume that all of these wondrous ideas you're picking up will be relevant for your here-and-now reality. But write them down anyway. Years later, you may be amazed to discover, when looking through these ideas, that you were getting answers to questions that didn't even arise until later! Just as often, these insights offer a perfect solution to something you've been puzzling over in the here and now world. So write them down, and don't assume you'll be able to rethink these nuggets of insight later. You didn't think them up this time and you won't be able to again later, so get them encoded or lose them.

Breath and Energy Are One

There are many ways to work with energy, but none better than breath. If only breath work cost a tremendous amount of money and took years to master—there might be more respect for its amazing power. But it's free, and it's something you can experience within forty-five seconds.

EXERCISES FOR BREATHING
INTENTION INTO YOUR BODY

On the wings of breath, you can breathe anything into your body. Breath infused with intention can indeed imbue the body with whatever you choose; it's a wonderful practice. You can breathe joy, love, courage, creativity, healing, or anything else into your body by holding your intention in mind, anchoring yourself in the emotion of the energy you're bringing in, and then, on a deep inhalation, picture this energy being encoded in your body. Breathe this energy deep into your core. Hold your breath for a moment and imagine your lungs sending this energy into every cell in your body. On your exhalation, send out this awakened energy as the expression of who you are. Do this for several breaths and realize that every cell in your body that is being born in this moment—and there are millions of them every minute—is encoded with this energy you're inhaling. Now sit with this awakened energy and let it be.

Many other breath exercises have been developed for various benefits. Try these two for starters.

Calming Breath Exercise: Andrew Weil teaches this simple practice. First, place your tongue on the roof of your mouth; this connects an inner circuit of energy. Keep your tongue connected this way throughout the exercise. Breathe in through your nose for a count of 4. Hold it for a count of 7, then breathe out lightly through your open mouth for a count of 8. Repeat this cycle four times. That's it. It only takes about forty-five seconds, but it utterly transforms your experience of the energy of the moment. Use this technique when you feel anxious and need to calm yourself, or if you can't sleep. This practice can actually lower your blood pressure on the spot.

Circular Breathing: Sit with a straight spine. Place your tongue on the roof of your mouth and, as you breathe in, imagine that you're pulling energy up the front side of your body, from your tailbone to the top of your head. On your out-breath imagine that you're pushing the energy over your head and directing it down the back of your body to the base of the spine. Up the front side on the in-breath, and down the back side on the out-breath. After several laps in this manner, reverse direction and pull the energy up the back side on the in-breath and down the front side on out-breath. Now stop and feel.

In this exercise you are running higher mental energy by opening the energy centers from the base of your spine to the top of your head. Picture yourself opening up to more space for the energy to exist in, easing anxiety, relieving the feeling of compression in too tight a space. Circular breathing creates spaciousness within you.

You can expand on this exercise to breathe from the top of your head to the soles of your feet. Picture yourself sending energy all the way down through your body, through your feet, and into the earth. On your in-breath, picture drawing energy up through the earth, through your feet, up the back side of your body, to the top of your head and then into the heavens. On your out-breath, picture drawing the energy from the heavens, through the top of your head and back down the front side of your body, through your feet and into the earth. Repeat this cycle for several laps and then reverse the direction.

Now settle your attention into your heart. Picture the energy from the heavens meeting and merging with the energy of Earth, swirling together in your heart. This meditation promotes creative fertility—something will be born from bringing heaven and earth, the yang and the yin, together. And it will arise in your heart.

Public Speaking: Stage Fright and Stage Presence

Breathing and visualization often work well together. One good moment for them is when you're about to speak in public. Many people have a fear of public speaking, so this is a useful practice.

While standing in front of a group of people, who doesn't feel a tremendous amount of energy? Thoughts are energy; attention is energy. A crowd of people is looking right at you, creating an energy field that can be felt. If we had some type of device that could measure energy, we'd see that the most intense energy in the room is exactly where you are standing! All that attention, all those eyes, all those thoughts, all focused on you. Is it any wonder you feel energy when you are in front of a group? Wouldn't it be unusual if someone said they didn't experience energy in front of a group?

Of course there's energy here. Instead of denying the energy, or trying to ignore it, picture yourself riding it like a surfer riding a wave. Don't wish the wave away, ride it and give the energy back to the audience. Charismatic speakers vibrate with the group mind. Breathe into the nervousness—not to get rid of the energy, but to be one with it and give it back to the audience. You'll think you were just handling your nerves; they'll think you are an energetic and alive speaker!

INTUITION

When you're in the heightened energy of the fifth level, you are especially open to your intuition—those flashes of insight that seemingly come from nowhere. Insights, intuition flashes, sudden knowing, genius-like perceptions: call them what you will. But it's important to understand that intuition is not just heightened intelligence. It's not like super-rational thinking; it's supra-rational, on a different level. This could be called direct knowing.

To develop your intuition, follow the subtle promptings you spontaneously receive. Learning to listen to the subtle guidance of intuition is like noticing a wind that opens a door and makes you wonder whether there's some significance to this occurrence.

That happened to me in my writing cabin last summer. I was working on this book—this section, on intuition—when the cabin door opened with a puff of wind. I had just been forming thoughts about how to listen to the unasked-for guidance that nudges our consciousness. How could I be writing about this topic and ignore this unusual occurrence? I got up and went through the open door, which led me to the main house where I found my wife frantic, having been locked out of the house by her two five-year-old grandchildren! For no reason, I appeared on the scene just before it might have turned bad. Did I consciously think, "My wife is in trouble, I better go help"? No, I just showed up for no apparent reason other than a puff of wind opening a door while I'm writing about intuition.

A more dramatic example of this "knowing beyond knowing" was revealed to me years ago while living in Hawaii.

Laurie and I were living in our Volkswagen bus in a remote spot on Maui, out past the Seven Sacred Pools. Our days were idyllic. For our morning shower we walked down the road and up a creek to a tropical paradise waterfall and pool. Huge, lacy white butterflies graced the scene, and here we bathed, swam, and sat to start the day. I described our lifestyle in letters to my sister Lucy back in Seattle, mailing them from the post office in Hana, where we went weekly to pick up our mail. It must have sounded tempting.

On Thanksgiving Day, Laurie and I decided to visit the Seven Sacred Pools, so we started the van and headed down the abandoned seven-mile dirt road to get there. Absolutely no one was about. Halfway there, my hands jerked to the right on the steering wheel. It wasn't my intention, but I suddenly found myself pulling off the road onto a remote beach where I'd never stopped before. I circled our van around a tree in the center and admired the rugged beach. As we circled, I was amazed to see a girl standing next to a backpack. As we got closer, I said to Laurie with a start, "Wow, that girl looks just like Lucy," but of course it couldn't be because Lucy was back in Seattle. Well, it was Lucy.

Unbeknownst to me, she had written a letter announcing that she was coming to join us—but we hadn't picked up the mail that week yet. Lucy was in a free-spirited time of life and responded to the temptation by packing up and acting on it. She was surprised when she landed at the airport and we weren't there to meet her. Undaunted, she decided to find the land on her own, although she didn't have the address or directions, only a feel for where it must be. So she hitchhiked, but no one was around and this was as far as she got. Needing to regroup, she stumbled upon this deserted beach to rest.

I hadn't had any feeling of Lucy's presence. I was simply driving down an abandoned road when the steering wheel tugged on my hands like a dowsing stick. The outcome would have been entirely different had I simply adjusted the wheel back on course. On this Thanksgiving Day, I was grateful for this "knowing beyond knowing" that our intuition is all about. After the amazement and tears as we realized the impossibility of it all, we continued our journey to the Sacred Pools for a magical day of swimming and feasting.

Coincidences

If a friend mentions a book to you today, and tomorrow another friend mentions the same book . . . get the book. It's that game of looking for meaning in coincidences. It's your intuition that draws the connection and adds meaning to the coincidence, or at least looks for meaning. As you learn to pay attention to this voice, you gain confidence in knowing when this is one of those magical moments when guidance comes from information beyond the rational. We often learn of it retrospectively, noticing after some situation occurs that you had a feeling about it ahead of time. Learn to listen to these nudges of consciousness that come uninvited. They come of their own, and are not simply thought up.

After several months of helping friends establish their home and gardens on the back side of Maui, I was beginning to get restless. I was going through a spiritual awakening and one day I told my wife that I wanted to explore the island and see if there were other living opportunities available for us. When she asked what I was looking for, I responded: "I'd like to live with spiritually minded people. Nothing corny, just people who want to be closer to God every day."

We headed out to explore and a few hours later were in Lahaina, checking out the local scene. I got into a conversation with a young man who was painting a sign. When I asked him what he was doing on the island, he responded, "I live with a group of spiritually minded people. Nothing corny, just people who want to be close to God every day." The hair stood up on the back of my neck as I realized these were the exact words I had spoken to Laurie just a few hours earlier!

I take that type of coincidence as guidance, and at that moment I would have followed him anywhere. It was a commune that he led my wife and me to, inviting us over to meet his friends. This started our communal era; we lived and learned with them for most of a year and then returned to Washington to start the Rainbow Farms commune with a group of friends, staying there for another six years.

Insight and original thinking aren't an additive process, the result of accumulated knowledge. They often have the feeling of genius in that the information comes to you whole, complete, and absolute. You know without knowing how you know! As you learn to listen to this voice, it gives you original insight, fresh perspective born out of the moment rather than a reenactment of previously established behavior.

Giving personal astrology readings for over thirty years has provided me a wonderful theater for appreciating how this knowledge works. Astrologers draw on a large body of written knowledge about the meaning of various planetary combinations in people's lives. Astrologers have guidelines on where to look for these planetary energies as they play out in someone's life. These guidelines help direct your attention to a certain area of your client's life, but the possible specific interpretation of any of these archetypes could literally number in the hundreds.

I've grown to rely on intuition to guide me to what specific issues to talk about. The chart shows the general pattern, but for me, it's intuition that leads to my insights into exactly how an issue is playing out in this person's life. I assume that intuition will occur periodically throughout the reading. Not all of it, not at all. Much of my interpretation is simply competent astrology, but there are invariably several magic moments when I feel a sense of great certainty, a tug on the steering wheel of consciousness, and I just go with it. I've grown to appreciate those magic moments as the jewels of the interpretation. The chart and its traditional interpretation provides a good framework to rely on, but intuition leads to the special connections and insights.

It would be great if you could consciously open this doorway to knowing beyond what you could know, but that's not how it works. It isn't born out of conscious willful intention—its very nature is that it comes at unexpected times in unexpected ways. These insights come of their own volition. The key is to pay attention to them when they do come. Whenever you feel a twinge that says "Wait a minute, this has meaning," pay attention and this spontaneous guidance and insight is yours.

My wife Laurie and I lead group workshops at special and sacred sites around the world—Hawaii, the Yucatan, the Greek islands—and we've grown to absolutely trust our intuitive guidance to help us find those sites. "Planning" our retreats in Italy is an example.

Several years had passed since our last group trip. One day as I listened to a client describe her recent hiking trip in Tuscany, I felt a delightful stirring of interest. I had wanted to take our workshops in a slightly different direction and the possibilities of Tuscany thrilled me. I thought of a workshop that would include chakra study, but also hiking and exploring the culture, art, food, and wine of the region. I wanted a destination where the place itself would be as integral to the workshop as the material. So Laurie and planned a scouting journey.

This is not a tough part of the job. We hiked the Cinque Terra, delighting in the quaint towns and villages along the way. We feasted on the offerings of Florence and hung out in charming Cortona; we shopped for pottery in Sienna and loved the pervasive sense of history. But nowhere did I see or feel what I wanted for a workshop site. After a few weeks I gave up on finding the right place; I decided to quit trying and just enjoy the experience.

In Assisi, the home of Saint Francis and his legacy, we were enchanted by the village. The Basilica of Saint Francis with its fresco paintings is one of the most beautiful buildings in Europe. Beneath the church is an underground chapel where the saint is entombed. While sitting in the chapel in silent respect, I had the most delightful sensation: my heart warmed, filling my chest with tenderness and love. I suddenly felt healed of my childhood wounds that dated back to a negative church experience. This unasked-for gift was clear and distinct; nothing subtle about it. I sat in amazement. I had been in many Italian churches—that's where the art is—and although I can be reverent, I'm not prone to be devout. I wasn't sure what to make of this profound gift.

I spent the evening in the afterglow. And when we went back the next morning, again my heart chakra opened as I sat in the chapel. Now this was the type of place we were looking for. I was getting more than a twinge of intuition saying, "This is it." We decided to scout around and headed up a dirt road into the hills, and just outside of town we found a thirteenth-century castle renovated as an exquisite hotel. It was perfect, with abundant space, sanctuary-type grounds, ideal spaces for yoga practice, great food, a pool, and a view of the Basilica in the distance. We took groups there for the next two years and it was all I hoped it would be and more.

STATES OF HEIGHTENED AWARENESS

The brain functions on different frequencies with different activities. When you're awake, alert, and engaged with activities, you are in the beta state. When you relax, meditate, and get out of doing, you drop into the alpha frequency. The lower frequency gives wider gaps in the cycle, allowing for flashes of direct insight to occur. Driving on a familiar road or long highway can put you into the state of mind that is open to receive these sudden insights. Maybe they occur just as often for all people, yet some of us learn to listen to these gems of insight, and others just think of them as kind of weird! But they're only weird when you try to make sense of these gifts that come from beyond the realm that makes sense.

The purely rational mind discounts these aberrations from normality as not worth pursuing because they're not logical. But if that's your ultimate filter, you limit yourself to only that which can be contained within logic, which is not much of the universe at all! This choice to limit would indeed do just that, it would limit you rather than expand you.

Be rational where it is helpful to be rational, like in the "checkbook level of reality," where you need to learn to live within your means. That is rational, and helpful. But don't let this be the only level of intelligence you draw from. To only listen to your rational mind would cut you off from both your intuition and your passion, neither adhering whatsoever to what makes practical sense, but adding greatly to your sense of meaning and fulfillment in life.

We all have access to an intuitive connection to a larger intelligence, one that can bring us information that we didn't even know was available. Expect it. Make room for its subtle guidance in your mind, and pay attention to the clues revealed through coincidences and other nudges in consciousness that tell you "This is important." Liberate yourself from any "should," and approach with abandon that which you are truly interested in. By listening and sharing your insights with others through speech, art, dance, architecture, cooking, music, or just making your life a creative expression in the way you live it, you access more of that 85 percent of your intelligence that otherwise lies dormant.

Sustaining a balanced fifth level of consciousness gives you considerable freedom in life. Although you support innovative change in all areas of life, you are not actively against much, preferring to direct your energy toward your creative choices, of which you have many. You've learned that creativity is in the air, and when it presents itself as an intuitive flash, you act on it. You trust your authentic perception of truth, and this is the source of your freedom. Your life is not directed in any way by the dictates of the world around you; you simply choose how to participate. You are also free to express yourself in an uninhibited way whenever your creative insights present themselves.

Happiness at this level is experienced as the thrill of discovery—the electric kiss of fresh insight that startles you and quickens your breath—and the knowledge that you can express your truth.

SIX:
THE MENTAL LEVEL
OF HAPPINESS

Chakra: Sixth (the Third Eye)—the brow at the bridge of the nose.

Color: Indigo blue.

Core issues: Broad scope of mental activity, from the petty to the profound, the analytical to the poetic. Two general orientations: the logical, analytical, and objective approach and the imaginative, intuitive, subjective approach—both accessible to all of us, although we generally favor one over the other.

Signs of imbalance: Undisciplined mind. Escapism, illusion, ungrounded vision. Excessive daydreaming. Worry. Fear.

Signs of balance: "The mind is a wonderful servant but a terrible master": this saying describes your talent for gaining the best of the mental level without becoming a slave to it. You are able to rise above the noise of the everyday world to a place of inner refuge where your imagination leads you to sources of inspiration. You are sensitive even to the subtlest influences, and this you've learned to use for your advantage. You have learned to reside in your Observer state and often experience the bliss of pure observing. Your sensitivities to subtle vibrations allow you to commune with light, sound, and all of nature as sources of energy.

In the receptive mode, the sixth level brings you into pure observation, simply seeing things as they are. This is the witness point of consciousness, your Observer state, which is always simply watching. It sounds so easy to simply see things as they are, but it is almost impossible to stop attaching our storyline to our perceptions. To stay in the state of the Observer, stay out of judgment, analysis, and other story-making activities of the mind. See what you see without judgment.

THE OBSERVER

Suspending judgment is probably easiest when you're observing nature. You can go for a walk in nature and see without judgment the beauty of the weave of old and young trees, tall and short plants, birds and burrowing critters—you can simply see it all as part of the mix. Not so easy with people, particularly yourself. But that is the practice: see without judgment, without adding your storyline.

It's an interesting exercise to walk through a mall or a busy neighborhood and observe people as if you were viewing nature on a walk through the woods. Observe humans as you do nature and keep your judgment at bay as best you can. Pay attention to what you are experiencing, seeing and hearing, and observe your own thoughts as if they were little more than part of the landscape.

Seeing without Naming

The advice is simple enough: see and observe without judgment. This silent act requires no action at all—simply seeing and holding space for what you see without attitude about it—but it has a seemingly miraculous impact on those around you. It holds space for others to come into conscious awareness of that which they weren't aware of before.

When I was growing up, my mother had a way of looking at me when I was stretching the truth: without saying a word, she cut through all my bull. My wife is also excellent at this. She sees my "stuff," the less-than-honorable parts of my character, but she doesn't always name what she sees or bring it up to talk about. I just see her seeing me. Not judging me, but not being fooled by me, either. This has an unnerving yet healing impact on me. If she were naming my issues and nailing me for them, I could get defensive and accuse her of being critical—I would have something to fight against. But how do you fight someone simply observing you with no judgment about it? Well, you don't—that's the unnerving part. But it's healing for me as well, because it makes it easier for me to see parts of my character that I've been denying. Then I can come into acceptance of these issues myself, working on them at my own pace.

The Bliss of the Moment

The moments when you can see things as they are without wanting to change anything—when you see without judgment—open you to the bliss level of happiness. You see the pure joy in the play of life unfolding without thought about it, at least for a moment. These rare moments of insight give the feeling that things are as they are meant to be. You see the Divine perfection of it all. These glimpses into the profoundness of life are shattered when the ego tries to make sense of it. But in that moment before you try to understand it, you understand it.

You sustain these bliss moments by holding your analytical mind at bay. Give it an inch and it will reduce the bliss into something to think about, moving you out of the direct experience and into thinking about the experience. Breathe space into these moments, linger with them. Your anxious mind will get its way soon enough and to tell you all about the experience. But for as long as you can, treat the bliss as a special guest, one you don't want to offend with your mind's badgering questions that spoil the moment.

Sacred Awareness

The highest level of the urge for transcendence is found in sacred awareness. With this awareness you use your imagination to imbue life with sacred meaning; you expect it, court it, look for it, and find it. You become aware of a mysterious current of guidance that some would call the way of the Tao, some would call the great way, some would call the path. You are led to search for a way to see the Divine reflected through all of creation.

At this level, you have a strong desire to know your purpose in life—the purpose that goes beyond your profession. You are fed by activities that nourish your soul, which may set you apart from your more sensory-guided friends. You are often more comfortable with quality alone time than with the effort of trying to fit in with others.

Your path is guided by your sense of what aligns you with the sacred, and in the midst of this scarred and embattled world, you find your way to peace. Here you are using your imagination to its fullest.

THE MIND AND ITS THOUGHTS

Your mental level gives you the capacity to think, learn, and explore with your mind, to organize your thoughts and communicate them to others. This mental gift is what sets our species apart from all others. We have enormous mental capacity, for good or for ill, with seemingly no limits on what we can do with our intelligence. We can plot dastardly deeds, write great plays, design advanced weaponry, or develop healing technologies. The mental level can easily grasp one's full attention so that one's self-identity becomes rooted in thought. "I think, therefore I am": the dialogue of the mind with its self-talk is endless. Your mind always has very vital and important information that it believes needs your full and undivided attention.

The mind thinks—that is its nature. Thoughts are the mind's effervescence. You can't stop the mind from thinking, but you can learn to be discriminating about whether to listen to it or not.

We could say, "Your capacity to think is God's gift to you, what you choose to think about is your gift to God." Buddha said it this way: "You are what you think, having become what you once thought." And another teacher, Mirdad, offered this: "Think as if all your thoughts were written across the sky for everyone to read, for they truly are."

These sayings are poignant reminders of the formative power of the mind. What you think about literally shapes your life—therefore it's especially important to be discriminating with what you think about.

Imagine that your mind is hooked up to the mainframe computer that records all your thoughts. At the end of the week, those thoughts are classified and tabulated to show the amount of time you spent thinking about the various issues that occupy your mind. Now imagine that you could get your hands on this computer tally by visiting a public Internet site that stored the information for anyone to examine! Wouldn't you be more selective with your thoughts if you knew that everyone had access to them? Selectivity is a useful attitude to take while you're working with your mental "body." You're building your future life with your current thoughts, so make sure they are worthy of you.

It takes some mindfulness practice to come to know the true nature of your mind. It takes watching the mind run on and on with its constant prattle of late-breaking news. By watching the river of thoughts you begin to see how ephemeral they are, each all-important pressing thought to be followed by an equally important next thought—the rise and fall of the mind's natural effervescence.

In learning to watch your thoughts in this detached manner, you learn how *not* to follow each thought as if it were all-important. A good practice is to observe your thoughts as if you were watching a train pass before your eyes. Like a passing train car, each thought is there in front of you, and then the next thought is there. Practice not following each thought as it moves down the track—because here comes another thought that you can also practice letting go of.

EXERCISE FOR STAYING PRESENT

This simple exercise can be done with any object in nature or in your indoor environment. Start by paying attention to your immediate perception: look at a color in your surroundings and stay in your direct experience of that color rather than your thoughts about it. Do not immediately catalogue the information into your files that associate this color with a familiar, established group in your mind—named, categorized, filed away, end of transmission. Maintain the transmission by staying in the direct experience. You may find it awakens fresh discovery and insight, an unfettered view of things. Now take this exercise beyond vision in the literal sense. When you can extend this trusting of your direct perception, over and beyond listening to your thoughts about the perception, you open to direct insight.

Liberating Yourself from Tape Loops

When your mind gets hooked on a certain issue, it starts a "tape loop," repeating the same sequence of thoughts and eventually leading you right back to the start. Running a tape loop is different from problem solving. With true problem solving, you're working with an issue and making some progress. Maybe you have to return to the issue time and time again, but progress is being made toward eventual resolution. With a tape loop, no progress is made. You go through the same exact sequence of thoughts leading you right back to the beginning, where you will pick up the loop exactly as before.

These tape loops consume vital energy; you feel spent after getting caught in one. To break out of these circular thinking patterns, you need first to be consciously aware of what's going on. Without awareness, you may wander into one of these mental traps believing that it's a fresh go at the material. It takes awareness to see this occurring. But once we've noticed the pattern, what do we do next? Try these two techniques to liberate this wasted mental energy.

If the cycle has already started—you're stuck in a loop—interrupt it by grabbing any book or reading material close at hand and reading aloud, even at random. (It's rather awkward in social situations, but it sure works great when you're by yourself!) Of course it would it be better if you were to reach for something spiritually inspiring to read, but I've found that anything will do. You're replacing the loop with reading aloud, giving yourself a chance to clear your head and have a fresh go at it—in a productive way.

The second technique is subtle, but even more effective. You essentially notice an incipient tape loop—you feel it coming—and redirect the energy before it starts. This sounds easy, but is extremely subtle work: after all, how do you redirect a thought before it appears? Because that's essentially what you have to do: catch it before it starts. To develop this sensitivity over time, watch the whole cycle a few times from your Observer state. See yourself get pulled into the recurring thoughts and notice their effect on your energy field. How do you feel energetically?

By observing the loop and becoming familiar with the whole process, you eventually can sense the thought approaching, like a bubble rising in consciousness. You have to catch it at this most subtle level before it is even a thought. When you do, you can redirect the energy toward anything you choose. The energy that was being spent in the tape loop is now available to direct wherever you choose.

THE UNIVERSAL MIND

The universal mind is a composite of all the individual minds of humanity. All of us draw our intelligence from this same source.

Individual Cells in a Global Brain

It is said that we only use 5 to 15 percent of our brain's capacity. Doesn't this make you wonder what the rest of your mind is for? Perhaps it's not about your individual life. The mind is a social organism connected in the invisible web of consciousness. We are all transistors in the global brain, and the unused part of our mind is for collective mind activation. Meditating with a group is an example of how hooking up with others can often lead to deeper and more profound experiences than private practice. I've seen it happen at certain gatherings: when a group mind forms, the room becomes electric and, whether through the speaker or the audience, fresh insights are born.

The Internet is the physical manifestation of what is going on energetically. We are sending and receiving information from each other constantly. We all have access to the same web; what is knowable can be accessed. If the information is out there in the collective, you have access to it through your intuition.

"They Stole My Idea"

How many of us have had a creative idea and not followed through on it, only to realize that a year later somebody else has just done that very thing? If you decide not to write the book, you can go read it next year—written by the person who did follow through on the inspiration. Creative inspiration and great ideas come from the collective mind; they're not received by just one person.

We are all cells of consciousness in the greater mind of humanity, and at this level, we have access to the greater intelligence of humanity itself.

Zeitgeist: The Spirit of the Times

A beautiful word meaning "spirit of the times," *Zeitgeist* is the spirit that animates a culture's changing themes. Think of it as the collective wind blowing through the universal mind, inspiring the ideas that come to many people at the same time. Have you ever noticed how often a theme emerges and many people act on it simultaneously? It's common in Hollywood, where sometimes many people simultaneously have the idea for a certain movie theme or plot. Often Nobel Prizes are given to more than one researcher, sometimes many, who acted on the same idea at the same time, but independently of each other. These examples hint that there are collective ideas whose time has come, and whoever acts on it first gets the credit.

It's not just special people who have inspired moments. What makes the difference is that some will follow through on the inspiration and some won't. Some catch hold of an idea and ride the Zeitgeist current for all it's worth, but many let the creative inspiration pass by, doubting for whatever reason that they are the right person to follow through on it.

Sometimes the choice is deliberate and circumstantial. For example, imagine that one day while shopping in a supermarket, a woman with a busy, successful, happy life conceives the idea of manufacturing sanitized hand wipes for grocery carts. She may not wish to exert the energy to create them, but she can still support the received inspiration and know that they will appear in her grocery store soon enough. Or she can pass her inspiration along to the right person, one who is in a position to act.

Meditation: It's Not What You Think

To be skillful in the mental dimension, meditation training is advised. Nothing can get you back to the clear light of your Observer faster than a session of mindfulness meditation. Following your breath, letting go of arising thoughts—nothing works better. Pulling your attention back to breath and nothing more gives you the discipline you need to pull your imagination out of unhealthy zones. It's the surest way back to center, and it stabilizes you in the transcendent realms. Without the ability to pull back and observe, how would you know if you are using your imagination in a healthy way or not? Without your Observer to notice when you were being swept up on some unhealthy current, things can seem real when they really aren't.

MINDFULNESS MEDITATION

In this meditation you center yourself and become aware of the nature of mind. With this meditation you'll follow your breath exclusively as best you can. Sit in a comfortable position and start noticing your breath: that's it. With each in-breath notice the subtle rising, and with each out-breath notice the subtle falling of your energy. Listen to the sound of your breath, notice the sensations, and follow the subtle rise and fall of your energy. Practice this for several minutes and you will experience its value.

The directions here are simply to follow breath and let no other thoughts come in. This is impossible, as it turns out, but try it anyway. Each time you find yourself drifting to a thought other than paying attention to your breath, notice what's happening and gently pull your attention back to your breath. Notice that you can't stop your mind from thinking; that's what the mind does. "I have to pee." "I'm hot." "I'm cold." "I wonder what my child is doing?" "I should call my friend." On and on it goes; you can't stop it from happening. That's why we call it a mindfulness meditation; you become aware of the nature of mind.

This meditation is particularly frustrating at first because of how impossible it seems . . . you can't stop your mind from thinking and indeed, that's the point. But you do become more centered simply through the discipline of staying with the practice for five or ten minutes, and you also become aware of the insubstantial nature of your thoughts. When they arise, you learn how to let them go, even though they constantly demand your attention.

The meditation is useful in itself to demonstrate the nature of the mind, but the value goes beyond the actual practice. It becomes even more valuable at other times of day. Anytime your thoughts are moving in a direction you don't want to go, you can focus on your breath and the thought is gone! No need to analyze it, follow it, or think it through, it's just a thought that spontaneously arises whether wanted or not, and you simply learn to let it go. Ah, inner happiness returns.

Isn't it interesting that thoughts come in language? Thoughts are molded by words, heard inside yourself in the context of the language you speak. But perceptions do not come with the constraints of language. When the analytical mind labels the perception, there is language with the emerging thought. So lengthen the time between perception and thought, widen the gap, and linger in the perception.

Visual art, too, transcends language. It doesn't require words to communicate. While observing a painting, sculpture, collage construction, or other visual art, you can stay in the pure perception mode and let yourself be impacted by what you are seeing.

Light Beings Feed on Light

Awakening to your sixth level of consciousness is often accompanied by acute sensitivity to light. Your energy field, also called the "subtle body," is activated by light and can absorb energy directly through sensing multiple hues of light throughout the day and the year. In this noticing of the change in color and light, there is a quickening of the breath, and in this moment you are being fed by the light. Just as your body transforms the food you ingest into energy and body matter, at the sixth level, you transform light into subtle energy.

This sensitivity is often felt regarding the quality of lighting for various activities throughout the day. People with this sensitivity adjust the light to help set the tone for their activities: a different ambiance for watching a movie, working in a studio, preparing a meal in the kitchen, or eating the meal at the dining table.

You can facilitate the stirring of this inspirational level of consciousness by playing with light. Watch a sunrise or a sunset when the colors are richest, and imagine that you are drawing energy from the light and color. Your appreciation for it, your love of it, awakens the pathways to receive light as energy.

Do you feel like you're making up this sensitivity? Don't be concerned that it's just your imagination—that's the point! Training your imagination to do you some good is the purpose here.

COLOR WALKS

A wonderful method for activating this stage of consciousness is to take intentional color walks—a stroll in any environment that holds the prospect of plenty of color. Your focus on the walk will be to note the colors you see and then to dwell upon them—essentially absorbing the essence of the color into your being. Experience the color for a moment as you engage it, then move your attention fully to the next color that draws your attention. As your mind drifts to the details of your life, gently pull your attention back to color absorption and you will feel it as a recharge. You are ingesting energy of the most subtle sort.

IMAGINATION

Imagination is more important than knowledge. For knowledge is limited to all we now know and understand, while imagination embraces the entire world, and all there ever will be to know and understand.

—ALBERT EINSTEIN

The imaginary realm is within the mental level, and at its best it connects you to inspiration and vision. Artists court their muses and sources of creative inspiration. Spiritual seekers court their guides and guardian angels for spiritual inspiration. Both are using imagination in such a way that summons and manifests inspiration and vision from activity in the imaginary realm. Vision starts with creative imagination and then becomes reality. First you imagine a future garden in your mind's eye, then you bring it into manifest form. First you hold the vision of the quality of life you want to live, then you bring it into reality.

What a gift, this imagination! Here you are in this world verified by your senses, and even with your eyes open you can imagine being in another time and place. Imagination is not locked into the here and now. With imagination you can conjure up memories, picture what colors might look good in a room, imagine what clothes to wear for an event, dream up creative projects at home or work, envision an ideal romantic evening, get lost in a creative project, contact your spirit guides, and enter into sacred activities of all sorts—these are all active ways of using imagination to enhance and enrich your experience.

But all is not bliss with your imagination. It can get slippery out there in fantasy land! Your imagination can add so much to your life if handled masterfully, but it can create such havoc if let run loose. So yes, caution is advised when entering these waters. Your imagination is the magic carpet ride that can take you anywhere. That's the problem: anywhere includes many places that are troubling to a soul adrift in the world beyond self with no training or preparation. It takes some experience to navigate in the imaginary realm and learn to stay anchored in the Observer level of consciousness. For your Observer has got to be your home base—the place where you pull back all activity, including the mind's activity, and simply observe.

Monitor Your Imagination: Inspiring or Draining?

How do you know if what you're imagining is healthy or unhealthy? A simple method is to use yourself as a barometer of the experience and read the results on your energy field. When you come back from some imaginary wandering, ask yourself, "How do I feel?" If you're energized and inspired, the indications reveal this is to be a healthy use of your imagination. If you come back from your wanderings and feel drained, depressed, or fearful, your barometer reading is unhealthy for you. You need to pull your attention out of that which has this depressing effect and aim it at something that inspires you.

As an example, notice how you feel energetically after imagining that you have a specific health problem. Using yourself as a barometer, you can see how negative imagining drains your energy field. Conversely, if you're imagining soul connections to loved ones who have passed and you're feeling inspired by them, notice how this registers on your energy field. Learn to engage your imagination in ways that inspire you, and disengage from the ways that deplete you.

Your imagination links you to the collective images of humanity, the high and the low. Picture a great library that contains all of the images that are possible for humanity to imagine, from the inspired to the disturbing. Now pretend that you are in this library, reading something that really creeps you out. What's the obvious advice? Put down the gruesome material and go engage something more rewarding. Both are available in the same library. You learn to navigate by honoring what is empowering for you and steering clear of that which drains you.

Awakening to this dimension gives you access to the entire lake of human consciousness, the sediment and the clear water. Any technique to intentionally get to the clear water will work. You can meditate, read sacred literature, pray, go for a walk in nature, light a candle for the suffering in the world, or simply ask that you receive guidance from your highest source. Any intentional method to connect you to that source will do just that. For the less metaphysically inclined, getting clear might entail an athletic workout, or a run, or a private round of golf, gardening, or even chopping wood.

If you find yourself in the muck, first consider that it might not be your muck, it could be just the muck from the sediment level. When you attach moral messages to the world of images, you can even feel guilty or shameful about sexual fantasies, driving you further into the muck. Shake free of the morals and ethics and consider it from another point of view: how skillful are you in navigating these imaginary waters? You need to do whatever works for you to connect you to the clear water, the source of inspiration. It is your intention that is important, so follow whatever you are led to do, but do something to get out of the muck first, and then make your considerations.

Swimming Beyond the Ropes

Imagine a beautiful swimming lagoon off the ocean. The protected inlet provides safe and gentle water. Imagine part of the lagoon roped off with buoys enclosing the safest swimming area. Outside of the buoyed-off area are mysterious waters revealing beautiful underwater sea caves, but also treacherous currents that could pull you out to sea. It is advised to stay within the sheltered waters, but the adventuristic want to explore the sea caves, and the foolish get swept out to sea. It's in your best interest to know the nature of these currents.

Your ego is the lifeguard in the roped-off area, but it can't protect you outside of its realm. Your Observer becomes your lifeguard in the transcendent realms. If you can stay in touch with your Observer, who is silently watching the show, assume you are safe.

At this level the separate ego identity is meant to dissolve as you become aware that you are part of something much larger than your personal self.

Re-envision the Past

Imagination is not locked into time; it can summon images from the past as easily as from today or the future. One of its great uses is for harvesting wisdom you might have missed along the way. We would like to think that everything has a reason, but as we live our lives, we don't always see the spiritual lesson in the moment. Maybe we're hurt and just grabbing for a life preserver, or maybe we're just oblivious to the deeper soul message conveyed through some incident, but often we miss seeing the wisdom in the moment. It is through imagination that we are able to revisit lost opportunities from the past to harvest the soul wisdom found there.

Imagine yourself as a spiritual detective scouring the past for clues of buried wisdom. Look upon confusing or upsetting memories and ask of yourself, "What was my soul trying to teach me that I missed then, but now may see?" or "How may I become a better person by seeing this in a different way?" If your intentions are honorable, you can always find wisdom buried in your past.

This found wisdom doesn't just have archaic value for resolving the past; you'll find that it has applications today. By re-envisioning your past, you change the matrix that your current reality is based upon. This recaptured wisdom changes the dynamics of your involvements in the here-and-now world, and all of a sudden, it's as if you'd been making wiser decisions all along.

Daydreaming and fantasizing are natural functions of your imagination, and how you use these are up to you—which currents will capture your fantasy? Where will you send your magic carpet? Where will you allow yourself to go? The collective zones are filled with as much weird energy as inspired energy, so it's wise to be discriminating. When you're in fantasy land, the rules change and what seems so real might not be at all.

Examine Sexual Fantasies

Sexual fantasy is an expression of the imaginary realm linked with the second level of sexual desire. Fantasy fueled by desire, desire activated by fantasy—they can be delightful or obsessive; you decide. Sexual fantasy is an example that most are familiar with; it shows how the imagination can piggyback with other levels, for good or for ill.

Subtle Plane Ethics

Basically the rule is this: you wouldn't partake in any activity with another without that person's implied consent, and the same ethics apply at the subtle imaginary level. To be ethical, even in these subtlest of realms, would be to seek permission from another before engaging in a fantasy together. Obviously you don't have to call the person up and ask permission. At least not on the telephone. But perhaps it would be wise to ask this person's permission inwardly. If your image shuts down, that's the answer—respect it.

Ask yourself, is your fantasizing honoring or dishonoring the other? If this seems like an overly meticulous approach to you—after all, it's just a fantasy—remember that energetically it's the same at all levels. It's one thing to engage another person's energy without their consent. It's a completely different thing to truly share something with another; it can open the door for sacred sharing, even at this nonphysical level.

Let's look at a few more examples of the imagination level blending with other levels.

Try Pre-performance Visualization

This application is well known among people in performance competitions: visualizing the successful completion of the event ahead of time markedly improves performance. Athletes learn to envision the ideal shot, businesspeople picture the successful completion of a campaign, even a person selling or buying a home can do a pre-performance visualization of the sale, and the odds are improved with this help from the imaginary realm. Of course this doesn't lead to 100 percent success, but it does improve the odds and is well worth the effort.

I coached Little League baseball for several years when my boys were young, and I found that pre-performance visualization was helpful in teaching children how to hit a baseball. I noticed that the players who were struggling with it always had a the deer-in-the-headlights look in their eyes while they were up to bat, and their breathing pattern reflected the panic—

shallow "butterfly breath." Their entire pre-performance visualization was based on the fear of striking out. With all their focus on this fear, naturally they struck out more often than not.

Along with the mechanics of hitting, I taught them breath and pre-performance visualization, without using those terms, of course. We talked about stepping up to the plate with a strategy. The advice went something like this: "While you're standing there, look out at the field and find places where there aren't players, the big open spaces. Picture in your mind where you think it would be good to hit the ball and imagine how good it would feel to do it. Breathe slowly to calm your nervous energy. Breathe into your belly and then slowly exhale before you step up to the plate. When you're in the batter's box, stay with the deep breathing, be aware of your feet digging into the earth and picture that you are drawing the earth's strength up through your body. Feel how good it will feel to hit the ball, and do it!"

Send a "Higher Mind Communiqué" before the Meeting

You can also try pre-performance visualization for an upcoming meeting that you want to work out favorably. When you've scheduled an important meeting with someone, spend a little time in meditation beforehand and send your intentions to the higher mind of the person you'll be encountering. It works best when you are free of all ulterior motives and are seeking something in everyone's best interest—so get free of guilt by shaking off any ulterior motives you may harbor and do your best to come from your highest place. Now imagine the meeting taking place: you are communicating your intentions to the other person, who you find to be open to your ideas. Open yourself to receiving from the other person, just as you want that person to be open to receiving from you. Feel the satisfaction of reaching an agreement that is mutually beneficial. Be thankful and close your higher mind communiqué.

Send Healing Energy from Afar

While sending a prayer to a friend in need of healing, instead of focusing on the wound or illness in the process of healing, send the image of the healing complete and the person enjoying life again. This type of energy healing helps activate the person's health matrix. It removes the image of the wound from the energy field altogether and empowers the image of health for your friend. It can do tremendous good, even helping to jump-start the healing and recovery.

Picture Your Relationship When You're Not Together

When you and your partner aren't together, the time you spend picturing your partner is just as important as the time you actually do spend together. The quality of time you spend inwardly with a relationship actually sets the stage for your experience when you next come together. Focus on your disappointments with the relationship, and your next encounter will start disappointingly. Focus on the delightful aspects of your relationship, and it will start delightfully.

Liberate Yourself from the Fear Zone

Here we're referring to the fears you simply make up—the kind that serve no real purpose, unlike natural fears such as jumping from a snake to avoid potential danger. With made-up fears, you're dwelling on things that aren't actually happening in your life, but are possible to imagine. And oh, what we can imagine when we hook into the fear zone! Of course these fears are unhealthy; every clue from your being is yelling "Stop, this is painful." But it's like an addiction for those who are prone to it, and the strangest of mistresses to be seduced by.

Don't Feed the Monsters

Instead of feeding the fear monsters with your attention, try imagining something else, anything else. If you pull your attention out of the fear, you take the life out of it, literally. Don't wrestle with the dark; turn on a light. If it's all just imagination anyway, why not imagine something interesting?

Picture being in a dark room. You want to get the darkness out of the room, so you start shoveling it out, shovelful by shovelful, with great determination. You're not making any headway, but undeterred, you redouble your efforts. A friend comes by and wants to go to a movie, but you can't, you're busy digging the darkness out of your room. This goes on for a while, and eventually a light-hearted friend comes bouncing into the room and says, "Hey, it's dark in here!" as she flips on the light. And the darkness is gone.

To extricate yourself from the fear zones, recognize that it's your imagination that's feeding you this unhealthy information—and this you do have some control over. First unplug the life force that is feeding the fear: your attention. Without attention, the fears don't exist. Next, visualize something that focuses your imagination, such as the colors of the rainbow, a favorite memory, or the image of a favorite deity or spiritual buddy. This simple exercise will direct your imagination into something healthy, and just as important, out of something unhealthy. Vow to not fall prey to the incessant chatter of the fear monster.

Monitor Your Image Diet

What are the sources of your image diet? With any diet, the intent is improved health. An improved physical diet leads to better physical health. An improved emotional diet boosts emotional health. An improved mental diet enhances mental health, and an improved image diet improves your psychic well-being.

Consider the sources of your images: for most of us the primary ones are television, movies, the Internet, books, and other media. In our era, media is the mythmaker. If you're not selective you'll simply ingest what the popular press dictates and become a product of its current campaign. But here you have a choice, if you wish to exercise it. Just as you learn to monitor your self-chatter throughout the day, you can practice the same discriminating awareness with images.

Begin to notice what types of images are placed before you, and what type of impact they have on you.

You can only learn what is healthy for you by direct experience. Other people's experience in these waters can give you a heads-up, but you learn through your own senses. What empowers you? What disempowers you? As always, these are your guidelines for health and happiness in any plane.

The son of a client of mine was going through a period of frequent nightmares about bad guys trying to get him. He was seven at the time and often woke up afraid, needing to talk about these night terrors. His mother made him a dream-catcher to hang over his bed to snag the bad dreams, and while this helped initially, the nightmares soon returned. When I asked her about her son's media involvement, she said all he did was play video games. When I asked her about the content of the games, she said she really didn't know—they were just kid games. I suggested that she sit down with her son while he was playing and observe the content. She did, and reported back that in the game her son was most absorbed in, bad guys indeed appeared out of nowhere, threatening to kill him. The player would have to kill them first to keep playing.

It wasn't hard to draw the connection: the images the boy was immersed in were getting into his psyche and the game was continuing in the dream realm, where he became one of the players. When his mom talked to him about the link between the video game and his dream world, somehow it helped, giving the boy a way to make sense of it and quell the fear. The mother also started more actively screening the images her son was exposed to, and this also helped.

Chant Mantras to Dispel Negativity

The chanting of mantras, or sacred phrases, works marvelously to break free of a fear zone. The sound waves amplify the healing effect as your attention is drawn to the words and phrases. Thich Nhat Hanh gives a mantra that you can use while walking: "Breathing in I calm my body; breathing out I smile." Try repeating this to yourself to liberate yourself from negative thoughts. Sanskrit chants have an impact beyond their translated words and the sounds themselves help you tune to the intention of the mantra. Perhaps the most famous is "Om Mani Padme Hum." Its literal meaning honors the jewel of the lotus flower, but when chanted it also invokes a powerful cleansing of impurities in mind and emotion and realigns you with your original nature. Another mantra, "Om Namah Shivaya," helps you honor the divinity within you.

NONORDINARY STATES OF CONSCIOUSNESS

Your imagination is a portal: here you leave ordinary states of consciousness behind and enter life on the other side of the looking glass, where saints and sinners frolic. Some people are even able to communicate with entities who have crossed over and those whose service remains on the other side. This is the astral plane, an interface realm between the beings on this side and those on the other.

In this realm you can contact your guardian angels, spiritual guides, and helpful ancestors. When you need help in your life, you can call on these spiritual buddies and they will be there to assist you. If you're trying to kick a habit or pull yourself up to a higher level, ask your guardian angels to help, and they will. When you're concerned for a loved one, send a spiritual support team to your loved one to offer strength and protection. This is much more helpful for your friend than sending them your worries. When you need support in important family decisions, ask a favorite ancestor to be present to help the family.

When listening to guidance from this level, how do you know if you are listening to a higher being or simply trickster energy? Use yourself and your well-being as a barometer. After your experience, is your sense of well-being enhanced or diminished? There's your guidance. There's no reason to entertain negative energy from this realm; there is so much good, loving, supportive energy to draw on.

Spirits Don't Have Bodies, but You Do

On your journeys to other dimensions, you may contact spiritual beings who know nothing of the limits of being in a body. They don't need sleep, rest, or food, but you do! If you're connecting with any such beings, they will run you ragged 24/7 until you get it: *you* are the one who must define the boundaries you need to maintain a healthy body. Don't expect your spirit buddies to define them—it's not their department.

It's not rude to establish a schedule with your spirit buddies. If you have a busy life, it's fine for you to claim your need to schedule them in. You can honor the contact by creating special time and space for the connection in your life. You might say that every night from ten to eleven o'clock you'll have pen and notebook in hand. Then honor the commitment, and you'll find your channeling buddies will likely do the same.

Until distinguishing between healthy and unhealthy imaginary activity becomes somewhat automatic, you have to learn the ropes by raw experience. After getting caught in negative currents a few times, you learn to avoid these whirlpools, and you aim instead for the nectar this realm holds: inspirational guidance. If you find yourself in a negative zone, remember that your attention is guiding your experience. Unplug your attention to the negativity and it disappears. Drop your attention into your heart, ask that you be filled with loving, lifting energy—and that's exactly what you'll get.

Asking for Filters

If you find yourself picking up unwanted energy or information, try asking your higher self for the filters of your choice. It helps.

I recall my own early direct experience with filters. At the time I was first learning to open my sensitivity through spiritual practice, I was working as a waiter. Although it sounds silly, I found that with my new openness I was getting way too many messages from the customers, when all I wanted was their sandwich order! Opening up to intuitive information wasn't always helpful, I learned, and in the wrong situations it was confusing. I was too sensitive at times when it wasn't helpful, and I just felt weird.

I wanted to keep developing my sensitivity, but I had to ask my higher mind for filters if I was going to stay healthy in my family, my work, and my community. The first filter I requested was that I only wanted information that would be helpful, loving, and lifting. There are all types of energy out there and I couldn't run the sixth-level energy if I was carrying around images of darkness and depravity. Does all this shadow material exist? Certainly, but it would hinder my ability to stay open and available to others. The second filter I asked for was that I wanted to receive information about others only when they wanted me to have it.

This helped. When I had a particular focus, such as being a waiter, or coaching a kid, or meeting someone at the store, I wasn't Mr. Intuitive Guy. But if someone was asking for guidance, then I would gladly be of service.

Communicate with Other Levels of Intelligence

For many of us, the idea of communicating with other levels of intelligence conjures an image of communing with a plant and believing that its spirit will help us know its needs. Or holding a crystal that we believe will help us align with our intentions. Or asking an oracle for guidance and trusting that if our intention is to receive higher guidance, then that's exactly what will happen. At this level we are able to look for sacred guidance and find it. We can go to a special sacred place on the earth with the intention of hearing our highest truth and trust that we will get it. We can engage in any activity we deem sacred with the intention of finding our highest guidance—and it will be there.

We trust in a level of intelligence beyond our own, one we tune in to for guidance. The answer to our question comes in whatever emerges in us after seeking guidance. What we trust is what arises in us. It's not so much the precise words and specific directions we might receive, it's our own inner response that we want to pay attention to. We trust that what arises in us is the sacred guidance we seek. We do our part by asking for this guidance with reverence and respect. Then we trust what arises in us as a result.

USING VISION TO HELP MANIFEST YOUR GOALS

Visualize what you want to experience, then imagine what it would feel like if it were already true. Next, sustain the awakened joy of your wish-coming-true into current time and live as if it is already true. Then allow it to become true.

With this technique, you link your imagination with your emotions, adding potency to your goals and the process of realizing them. First focus your mind on imagining a specific ideal or goal. Then take it a step further: enter into the emotion of how it would feel to successfully achieve that ideal or goal. This visualization moves you beyond simply yearning for something. When you yearn, you are linked to an imagined future state, not to the here and now—happiness is elsewhere, not here. But when you create the emotion of the achieved goal for yourself, you bring that happiness and satisfaction into the present. Practice it, and you will learn how to enter into the enjoyment of the eventual manifestation of your vision.

This exercise also helps ensure that your goal-setting strategies resonate in your heart. You know your goals are in your best interest if your heart is in them. If you have trouble enjoying the emotion of realizing a goal or ideal, perhaps it isn't right for you. Tap into your heart level—and all the levels of your being—to bring your own wisdom to bear on your goals and ideals. That will allow you to maximize the power of this exercise.

Visionary Activity

The inventiveness of the awakened expression level combined with the compassionate vision of the mental level leads to the social visionary. This combination is idealistic and innovative; it yields the inventors of new paradigms, those on the leading edge of social visionary activity. They aim at what can be done. Thankfully we have the whistle-blowers helping to expose corruption, but fortunately we also have the visionaries who offer us ways to move forward in the here and now.

My family lived for a number of years in communal settings, and for us, the spirit motivating those years was visionary. At that time we saw cooperative living as a viable alternative to the typical nuclear-family lifestyle. I was motivated by simple ideas and advantages. For example, I wondered, why does every family need a set of tools and a (minimal) workshop, all duplicating the same resources and rarely used? Why not take all of those resources and put them together to make one really great workshop, and then share in its use? That was our basic vision: pooling our resources, cooperating to create a better quality of life. The commune was responsible for a farm, a restaurant, and children, which we all spent time with equally. Our law was consensus approval or no action. This empowered each of the fifteen people equally. It was a worthy effort that lasted for seven years until people's life paths led them in different directions.

Working toward your vision always holds it off into the future. Work from the vision and you make it present.

————————————

By learning to skillfully navigate in the mental realm you have enriched your possibilities for happiness many times over. You have learned how to steer clear of unhealthy images and feed yourself on that which inspires you. Being at home in this dimension greatly enhances your sensitivity on all levels. Physically, emotionally, mentally, and spiritually you run on a finer fuel than most, requiring you to avoid whatever is toxic for you at all levels. The upside of this sensitivity is that subtle healing techniques can bring you back to well-being. It doesn't take much to throw you off center, but it doesn't take much to bring you back, either. Your sensitivities to subtle vibrations allow you to commune with light, sound, and all of nature as sources of energy. Your acute awareness of the flow of energy gives you an uncanny ability to get out of harm's way just before trouble presents itself.

If imagination is going to lead you to fear or faith, choose faith. You learn that without guidance, your imagination can lead you to the best or the rest of what is possible, both in random measure. With direction, your ability to imagine is trained in directions that are uplifting, inspiring, and open to receiving guidance from the mystery that is life.

As you become balanced at the sixth level, you periodically slip into a state of pure awareness, the calling card of the seventh level.

SEVEN:
THE SPIRITUAL LEVEL
OF HAPPINESS

Chakra: Seventh—the crown of the head.

Color: Violet.

Core issues: Pure awareness, experience of the Oneness. Enlightenment. An awakened state.

Signs of imbalance: Inability to connect with reality. Disassociation.

Signs of balance: You have become a universal being, not by sacrificing the self, but by liberating yourself from attachments to other levels and anchoring yourself within the Divine. You no longer approach this state; you become absorbed in it. You are integrated at all levels, so you can participate in all of life smoothly, without being ruffled by the highs and lows that tug on you. You live with equanimity, accepting as sacred grace all that life places before you.

The seventh level is pure awareness. Not thoughts about awareness. Just awareness.

The word *absorption* aptly describes the process of experiencing the spiritual level. It is not so much *achieving* as *being*. You don't reach this state as a final goal; you simply drop all of the illusions that tell you it isn't here already. It is not really an effort, as effort is directed by the separate self. When you let go of all effort, your attention is reabsorbed into the Oneness, and your individual perceptions become creation taking delight in creation.

You can't earn this as if it were some special achievement, although efforts are necessary to tame the restless mind so that you can be absorbed into the fabric of the Oneness. Lack of effort doesn't imply just watching television, eating chocolate, and drinking beer! Your spiritual efforts, such as meditation and prayer, are important ways to help prepare yourself to receive Divine input. Then effort is set aside to let you slip into and merge with the Divine. Beyond becoming, it is being.

ABSORPTION

One doesn't need to be enlightened to have an enlightened moment, a moment of pure absorption. These precious moments of awakening are transitory, rather than a permanent new plateau. You may experience them as moments between time, between breaths, when eternity seems to open before you. A pebble thrown into a lake splashes and sends out rings, creates an effect for a moment, and then the water closes the hole and returns to its way. Your awakened moments are like this: they are quickly swallowed up by the many other dimensions of your being calling for attention. The window of insight into Oneness is quickly closed—at least it seems to be closed when your attention is elsewhere. But know the window is always open, always available to return to, always there. Be thankful of knowing that when you can once again quiet all of the distractions, you will again see with unfiltered vision.

The Value of Silence

Silence is one of the direct paths to experience the spiritual level. With silence, you can listen; you can absorb and be absorbed. There is a saying: "Silence is the true language of God; all others are poor translations."

EXERCISE FOR EXPERIENCING STILLNESS

Practice ten minutes or more of absolute silence daily. Do this practice gazing out into nature, or looking at a blank wall: the benefits are the same. Start by turning off all media, of course, but also turn off your inner media. Just sit and silently observe. No techniques to follow, no breaths to watch, no thoughts to monitor—just sit and observe. Quiet externally, quiet internally. Enter into the stillness of being. When you hear a sound, let go of identifying it as the sound of a particular thing, and picture it simply as sound waves moving through you. When your eyes notice something, picture light waves moving through you. Stay out of identifying and commenting inwardly on it; simply experience. This practice dissolves all feelings of separateness. When you quiet yourself, you can't help but feel part of the same fabric of all that you are experiencing.

Although it is characteristic of the spiritual level just to be in the awakened state without effort, we often need considerable practice on the way to that state. Some of us can readily go to the place beyond being entertained by our own thoughts, but most of us need the training of meditation to travel beyond the mind's constant babble. Without some sort of discipline for stilling the grasping, chattering nature of our being, all these yearnings and aimless thoughts will pull our attention to their needs. With a discipline, we learn to quiet the cravings and the noise. Then we can move beyond the practice to where true listening and true absorption can take place.

Grace

Grace comes as unasked-for, mostly undeserved, spiritual blessings that are bestowed upon us throughout our lives, often at times when we need Divine intervention most. Moments of grace affirm to us that the universe has a heart. As you experience life from the spiritual level, you are able to recognize and receive the signature of grace in life unfolding. Grace is constantly showering its blessings upon you throughout your life, and at the spiritual level you are open to receive its guidance.

To experience grace, cultivate a deeper appreciation of the magic moments: the beam of sunlight through the trees, illuminating with its warmth and light a special moment of fresh awareness. This is grace, an offering from beyond, affirming to us there is a spiritual level, and that opening to it is healthy, right, and natural. Experiencing grace is like experiencing coincidences with a heart. Grace feels good—it is warm and embracing. This is its measure, and an affirmation that something is watching out for you.

We all have special teachers, books, and guides along the way. For me it was in the mid-1970s and the book *Autobiography of a Yogi* by Paramahansa Yogananda. Reading the stories of the magical saints lit me up in a way I had never experienced before. After reading Yogananda I was on a spiritual high for months. Laurie and I were living in Hawaii and totally open to being guided by spirit. I found Yogananda the perfect teacher for me at that time.

A few years later we had moved to Seattle, where I opened a bookstore and astrology center. I had been in a prolonged cycle of the spiritual blahs—not depressed, but certainly not inspired. I was contemplating this while riding the bus to the store on a rainy, dreary day that matched my mood perfectly. I was trying to remember the last time I felt that warm glow I was missing. Reading *Autobiography of a Yogi* immediately came to mind. I remembered tears of joy while reading the book, and I vowed to reread it in an attempt to reclaim the magic.

And it worked. I buried myself in the stories all day and into the evening and this brought me right back into the spiritual glow for which I was hungering. What a different bus ride the next day—same rainy, bleak weather, but the sun was shining inside me, and it all looked wonderful. I remember chuckling to myself and thinking, "Thank you, Yogananda!"

Later that morning I was in a private consultation with a client when there was a knock on my door. I called out that I was in a session, and the person said that he had something for me and would leave it on the counter. When I finished my session, I found the brown paper bag he left, and looking inside, I discovered a framed eight-by-eleven photograph of Yogananda! I was stunned beyond belief with this treasure of grace.

Later in the day a man I knew came by and said that he had left the photograph for me earlier. When I asked him how in the world he thought to give it to me this day, he answered, "I just woke up this morning knowing as clear as can be that I was supposed to give this to you, so I did."

This was the most dramatic expression of grace I have received in this life. More often grace is subtle, like the right book showing up at the right time to strengthen your spirit. Or the many small ways throughout the day that spirit reminds you that you are on the right path. Grace is finding your way back to your path when you've gone astray. To live in grace is to receive its gift. Like a fire in the fireplace, it is always there to give its light and warmth when you return to the source.

An Inherent Order

At the personal levels, we discriminate, sort, and arrange to build order in life. It's a tough job, but somebody has to do it! From the spiritual level, you see an inherent order that already exists, revealed most beautifully in ecosystems. When you walk on a beach, you become aware of how exquisitely ordered it already is. At the personal levels, we might want to arrange things to our liking, sort and categorize by size and shape to get this place in order! At the spiritual level, we feel part of nature's weave, knowing that it is all perfect.

EXERCISE TO FEEL PART OF IT ALL

Go for a walk in nature with the intent of extending your self-identity to include all that you see. Notice that at first you feel separate from nature, as if it were something you're "looking at." Imagine that all you see is part of you. If it's autumn, notice the leaves turning and say to yourself, "My leaves are changing colors." See the breeze gently ruffle the leaves and say, "I feel the breeze moving through me." See the birds and say, "These birds are flying through my mind." Imagine all of this as you. See the birds flying through one part of your greater being and landing on another part of you. See the sunlight warming one corner of your greater self and feel the raindrops landing on your branches. See the insects flying in your air. Look at the sky and clouds as extensions of your mind. See your sunlight shining through your leaves. Enjoy your expansiveness. Feel the power, love, and joy of shifting your attention from separateness to inclusiveness.

Dropping Your Storyline

The spiritual level of pure awareness is far removed from your personal storyline. It's where you are absolutely disengaged from thoughts of your separate self. In the first stages of consciousness, it's imperative and appropriate to develop your personal story through the trials and tribulations, the successes and failures, the joys and sorrows of your individual life story. As you move up through the levels, your personal storyline has less and less significance, finally dropping away altogether at the seventh level, spiritual consciousness.

At the spiritual level, there is no one to become enlightened! Cutting loose even of the individual drive for enlightenment, you move out of your individual experience and merge with the Oneness that is now expressing through you.

When we are looking for individual enlightenment, we expect to wake up with the "I" suddenly aware of everything. Perhaps it has been our error that assumes that the individual self can attain such a state. It would be more fruitful to make the leap and consider this a collective phenomenon. Consider letting go of the "I" altogether and picture moving into our collective enlightenment.

This is the spirit of the Bodhisattvas—beings who have forsaken their individual enlightenment in favor of helping all humankind ascend to a higher vibration. To employ this in your own life wouldn't be to ignore your own awakening; rather it would be to dedicate your awakening for the greater good of all beings.

The Silently Awakened Among Us

Those who have awakened and sustained their spiritual level of consciousness are not necessarily obvious to us. We often think of spiritual beings as emanating a radiant glow—the unmistakable halo, the aura and all. But most who align with this level of consciousness become somewhat silent and invisible. Of course we still see them and hear them, but not in a way that prompts us to put them on a spiritual pedestal. The silently awake carry no spiritual trappings. We emulate them, and by doing so, become better people.

When you crave the mystical and phenomenal aspects of spirituality, it pulls you to the sixth level and the magical mystery tour that this dimension is all about. From the seventh level, all of this looks like neon lights casting an eerie glow of the undifferentiated light of spirit.

It is easy to get distracted by the neon lights and fantastic tales of spirit. It all sounds so special. Many people who are on top of the mountain of awareness are not even aware of their spiritual elevation. Angels and guides are messengers from the sixth level. You may wish to hear voices and see visions, when actually you become the voice and are the vision. You can't hear the voice if you are the voice. Vision doesn't come to you at the seventh level, it comes through you. At this level, creation is looking through your eyes to see itself.

The Process of Self-Inquiry to Discover the Truth of Your Being

The process of self-inquiry can be very helpful in liberating you from mistaken identity. Sit in contemplation and ask yourself, where is this person within me who I think I am? Start by taking inventory: ask yourself, "Am I my body?" No, if you are aware of your body, where does the awareness come from? Ask yourself, "Am I my emotions?" Again, no, because there is someplace within you that is aware of your emotions, so this couldn't be the source of you. How about, "Am I my thoughts?" And once again you will discover that there is some place within you that can observe your thinking.

This line of self-inquiry frees you from limited beliefs about who you are. Although you won't be able to identify yourself by anything you observe, you'll know some of the things you *aren't*! There is something within you that you can relate to as a sense of self, but it is larger than all of its functions. This self-inquiry creates a feeling of spaciousness as you become aware of how expansive your self must be to incorporate all of these dimensions and more.

Enlightened Today, Total Ass Tomorrow

We all get glimpses into the spiritual dimensions of life; it is part of our human heritage. But the spiritual level of consciousness has only been *sustained* by a handful of spiritual masters throughout history. Most of us are still working at balancing our other dimensions. When we are out of balance, energy gets pulled to the imbalance and we attract events that pull our consciousness to that level. It's not as if we awaken to higher-level energy and never again fall prey to human frailties of the lower drives! Not at all. Even states of consciousness that we call enlightenment are not sustained. One is more likely to bob in and out of the highest states of consciousness.

We can have such incredible spiritual highs one day, and then act out from such shameful lows the next. Don't be discouraged: it happens. We can expect to constantly be pulled down into the traumas and dramas of the lower drives, because it's their nature to pull on you. Learn to recognize your temporary slides. Witness them, vow to do better next time, and preferably smile at yourself and your follies. Have compassion for yourself. Feel good about yourself for at least recognizing the slip and know that you are growing in awareness.

Shortly after a period of intense spiritual awakening, I started offering weekend workshops for yoga and consciousness growth. After the first several of these workshops, I began to notice a pattern. The weekends were blissful; the returns from the weekends were not. I found myself putting on my spiritual best for these workshops—I was stretching a bit toward my best behavior. It seemed so incongruous that when I came home I often displayed some of my worst behavior. I would invariably do something crass, like indulge too much and pick a fight with my wife.

After I got a handle on this pattern I grew to think of it as "having been good for too long." I was hyper-vigilant about my behavior during the weekend workshops, but dropped my guard when I was back home. I have also observed this kind of stretch-and-snap-back pattern in my young grandchildren. Our grandson's first overnight away from his parents was a two-night stay with us, and he was on his best behavior. He pulled himself up to his best four-year-old self, and kept it together bravely, but we could see he was really working on being good. As soon as his parents picked him up, he let go of his self-control and began to act out the other side of his four-year-old self that he'd been pushing down. He'd just been good for too long, and I recognized the feeling.

All Methods Are Traps

On your journey from the physical to the spiritual, you need methods, tools, techniques, breath work, visualizations, prayers, sacred literature, and anything else that can help you rise above the separate nature of the personal planes. Reality coalesces around your perceptions and thoughts, and specific methods can help you move from the separateness of the lower stages into the expansive Oneness of the spiritual. The methods are helpful while they are useful, and they're certainly the place to begin, but there comes a time when methods actually stand in the way. When you're in Chicago, you don't need to take a bus to Chicago. While immersed in Oneness, you do not need to use methods to get where you are.

Perhaps you've found a prayer, a yoga posture, a passage in sacred literature, or some other tool that helps you invoke a higher spiritual state of awareness. If you become attached to the tool, you run the risk of ending up with an empty practice. The form and technique might be perfect, but spirit is larger than any technique and won't stay in the confines of any limited way of experiencing it. When spirit moves on and you're attached to the technique rather than the spirit it was helping you attain, you have an empty form, void of spirit. Reconnect with your hunger for spirit, more than your attachment to the form, and your practices will be rejuvenated.

As a child I was told by a friend while standing around a campfire that if I said the words "white rabbit" a couple of times it would make the campfire smoke move in another direction. I tried it, and when every once in a while it actually seemed to work, I felt affirmed—the phrase held the power of the smoke! Eventually I learned that smoke was attentive to a larger reality and wasn't subject at all to my magic words.

Spirit is like this. You go along in life and come across something that directly connects you to spirit: a prayer, a posture, a meditation, a teacher, something that your path leads you to that lights you up with spiritual energy. When you get caught up in improving the techniques of your connection, over and above the source itself, you are lost in the form. Spirit is always larger than any magic white rabbit trick you've learned. Stay open to this. When you use a technique, prayer, or posture to awaken to spirit and then let go of the form once you are there—that's perfect. Get off the bus.

When we think that it's only our form, our religion, our particular path or technique that connects us to true spirit, then we have limited spirit to the form, rather than using the form to spring into limitless spirit. That's like believing the sun shines only on one particular species of tree. None of the others are getting the true sun, only our type of tree is receiving the life-giving rays. Such a belief is lost in the form. The sun shines equally on all.

The Illusion of Separateness from the Divine

By definition, nothing can be outside the Divine Oneness; the Oneness includes everything. The whole embodies everything; nothing is outside of the whole. Anytime you are feeling separate from the Divine, realize the impossibility of that, and drop the illusion. Tell yourself, "This is Oneness being bored." "This is Oneness feeling separate from the One." "This is depressed Oneness." But know you are still part of the whole. Some people are more comfortable with a personal connection to the Divine and they would say, "This is God being bored." "This is Goddess feeling separate from the Goddess." And so on. But know in your heart, head, and soul that it is always illusion that leads to feeling separate; it is impossible to stand outside the One.

Don't Focus on the Wave, Focus on the Ocean

To activate your spiritual level of happiness, imagine your life to be a wave on the ocean, and then drop all singular focus on being a wave and shift your attention to being the ocean. Your life is the individual wave rising up out of the ocean. The spiritual level is letting go of all distinguishing features that make you separate and unique. By simply dropping all accounts of your personal story, you become absorbed into the Oneness of the ocean. You not only are connected to the ocean, you are the ocean—the immensity of being is just as much a part of you as your waveness. This gives you a sense of your being's continuity over the eternity of lifetimes; it even helps ease the fear of death.

DEATH

Should death be discussed in a book on the pursuit of happiness? Absolutely. A multilevel life turns its back on no aspect of life, including death, as part of our true experience. With death, the final illusion of separateness is dropped and the individual identity is totally absorbed back into the Oneness. Death is the great teacher of the nature of impermanence of the physical world; all that lives will die. Each wave that arises eventually returns to the ocean. The eternal, the now. The One as the many. The eternal nature of the Oneness, expressed over and over again in individual lives as moments in time. You are here for a while, and then you are gone.

When you experience the death of a loved one, this inevitable truth we all share breaks your heart. All defenses are shattered and your heart is laid open. In this sorrow and loss, your greatly expanded heart is open to more love. Death brings a family together in love in ways that everyday life usually doesn't. It's solemn, but it's love.

To allow the teachings of death into our life is devastating at first, as it brings home our worst fear. But if we stay with death as a teacher, and not try to stuff our feelings or avoid the experience, a profound openness occurs to the Oneness of life beyond time. Death is timeless in its relentless, eternal truth. Is there any other experience in life that is absolutely inevitable, for you, for me, for our children's children's children?

Death Opens a Door

There are often signs surrounding death, strange things that seem a little weird—or completely weird. Messages called by crows, a light coming on, doors opening, a picture moved, a breeze in a room with no windows open, all of it invoking this peculiar wondering: is that a message? Of course it is—the question is the answer. Listen to it. It will take you to places that don't make sense. That's the point. Be open to your higher guidance, and it will speak to you.

Dealing with a loved one's death is both tragic and a time rich with guidance. Death opens a door to fuller contemplation of life's meaning, and if we go with the lessons we always come out a deeper person for the experience. Often, an inner voice tells you what changes you need to make in your life, what directions you should pursue. Trust these messages. Messages from departed ones are not uncommon and come in many, many forms.

Our twenty-year-old nephew Bobby died last summer. At a gathering with the family at Bobby's house to support each other as best we could, stories revealed that after his death

Bobby had been visiting many people in his network of family and friends. His uncle Rick had been driving home thinking about Bobby and noticed the clouds broiling overhead. Feeling some kind of message, he got out his camera and photographed the fantastic scene. The photograph revealed a pattern in the clouds, forming in the heavens the exact same cross Bobby wore as a tattoo. A kind stranger helped his sister Patti out of a jam, and when she thanked him and asked his name, it was Bobby. A stray cat showed up at the bedroom window of one of his friends and demanded to be let in, insisting on attention. And of course, the cat's name tag revealed him to be Bobby.

I was back home contemplating all this when the light in my writing cabin inexplicably turned on by itself. After hearing all these stores, I just assumed it was a message from Bobby for the family. I grabbed a pen and wrote:

"It's all about the love, man, nothing else matters. I will be there for you. You will find my strength in your heart. Do not stay in the loss, I am still here."

Bobby's journals revealed him to be a seeker. He was the person friends would stay up late with, discussing life and the meaning of it all. He needed more tools. His dying touched off a flame of inspiration in me to write a book on living and dying and how to find happiness in it all—and thus this book was born.

Prayers to Those Who've Crossed Over

The communications you send to a departing friend, even if only imagined, are real and are received. Those recently departed and freshly stripped of the dullness of the senses are far more open to your silent prayers and thoughts. The inner blessings we send to one who has just died are immensely helpful for the soul navigating in new territory. These communications might occur only in your head and your heart, but they count.

Meditation can be a way of meeting a recently departed loved one. This happened for Bobby's mother, Michele. She received inner guidance that if she wanted to communicate directly to Bobby, he would meet her halfway. It took some weeks after his death, but she eventually found him through meditation—it was her way of meeting him halfway.

Although grief over the loss of a loved one is natural and healthy for the family of the departing soul, too much grief weighs on the soul's journey. Even worse would be negative, or greedy, thoughts about who gets what—these are very distressful to the departing soul, who would be better treated with prayers of well-being. It's important to experience grief, but temper your grief with blessing and support for your loved one's journey. In its own time and in its own way, your love for this person will once again fill the empty place that now only feels like loss.

The Quality of a Life Is Not Measured in Time

One can never be prepared for the profoundness of the experience of death. And on the ocean of life, waves take many different forms. Some waves curl along a calm bay and seemingly roll on forever. Some waves in a choppy channel arise magnificently, but for only the briefest of moments. Sometimes it is a child who dies of the strangest of circumstances, sometimes it is a friend in her prime, and sometimes death is the graceful dissolving into light of an aged parent. Death takes you beyond time. Don't fall prey to the illusions of thoughts such as "If I'd only had more time . . ." It is not about time, it is beyond time, into eternal rapport. Be with that place that isn't about time to be with your ascended loved one.

My grandfather was 105 years old when he died. People tell me it's wonderful that he lived so long. I never met him, although I almost did once. He lived on the East Coast, but he was coming to the 1962 world's fair in Seattle and was planning to stay with my family. On the day of his arrival I was abuzz with anticipation. His cab pulled up in front of our small, modest home, he got out, looked at the house, and without even saying hello, got back in the cab and left. We were all stunned. Later he called and said he couldn't stay in a place like our house; he had checked into a hotel downtown. I guess he stayed for the fair—but he never came to the house to meet us. His living to 105 meant nothing to me.

Our nephew Jacob was five when he died. People tell me it's terrible that he died so young. Jacob was the constant companion of our son who was just his age; they were practically raised together. At four Jacob became ill with a rare stomach cancer, and after a valiant battle, it became clear that he was leaving us. His health care workers had the wisdom to suggest that his parents take him home for his final goodbyes with the family. People began to gather at Jacob's house, realizing his imminent departure.

That last night, his parents warmly accommodated a slumber party for Jacob with his cousins, aunts, uncles, and closest buddies. It was a night I'll never forget. Bald-headed Jacob sat on the couch in the family room amidst a chaos of children and babies, games, toys, and food. One by one the kids came to Jacob to say goodbye—by sharing a toy, asking about his bald head, spending a precious moment. The party went on until everybody fell asleep where they dropped. During the night I woke up and looked at the surrealistic scene: Jacob asleep on the couch cushions with his parents, a jumble of bodies of various shapes and sizes strewn about the floor with mounds of sleeping bags and blankets. It felt lovely. Tribal.

In the morning it was evident that Jacob was getting tired. The extended family all said their goodbyes and we left. Shortly after, as Jake sat on his father Mike's lap, he said, "Goodbye, Dad." Mike asked, "Where are you going, Jake?" "I don't know, maybe to sleep." And then he died.

This experience touched us all profoundly. Life is absolutely impermanent; we never know when it will be our time. My wife Laurie began to wake our children up every morning with a hug—never taking a day with her children for granted. Our son who was Jacob's growing-up buddy now has a son with the middle name of Jacob. Jacob's heart lives on in our family.

Five years or 105 years—the number is no measure of the quality of the life and its impact on others.

We are all hanging by the slightest of threads to this life, and we never know when that thread will break. Knowing this is not meant to haunt us with pending doom; it can be the reminder to never take anything for granted. If you can keep it in your awareness that no one is guaranteed another day, it can help you stay aware of how incredibly precious this gift of life is.

Death Is a Hard Act to Follow

How do you follow death? It is sort of the final statement. Death is not the opposite of life; birth and death are both contained in our experience of life. Life experiences with a departed friend will continue in all dimensions other than physical. You will still have emotional and mental experiences with your friend—some anger, lots of love, intuitive insights, connections on the imaginary realm, and spiritual communion together. All of these dimensions are part of your life together, and they continue after death.

A multilevel life celebrates existence at all levels, not with a superficial happiness glossing over the challenging experiences, but with a profound respect for the full range of life and death that is our experience. During grief and loss, sorrow is appropriate, not happiness. But when you allow the full range of life experiences to touch you, when happiness returns it will be all the more profound.

THE CLEAR LIGHT

Just as clear light holds all the colors within it, at the spiritual level you embrace all of life before you. Your body, thoughts, emotions, and all the other levels become an instrument that the spiritual level expresses through. It's your instrument—play it well.

MEDITATION: RECEIVING THE CLEAR LIGHT

Imagine there are two suns. One is in your heart and animates you, the other sun is high above your head, and its light shines equally on everyone and all things across the planet. While in meditation, feel yourself being absorbed into the clear light of consciousness, the sun high above your head. Know that this is the part of you that has never been wounded or tainted by your life experiences. Breathing this energy through you reconnects you to this "source beyond wounds." Picture a beam of clear light energy coming down from the sun through the top of your head, connecting with the sun in your heart. Feel its clarity, its light, its illumination. With a deep in-breath, pull this clear light energy through the top of your head into your lungs and feel it heal and refresh all of your senses: your eyes, your nose, your ears, your taste, your touch—all purified and set right through interaction with this life renewing light.

As you breathe this clear light energy into your lungs, feel an instantaneous healing of emotional wounds with this infusion of light. As you continue to breathe, picture the lungs sending this incredible lightness of being to every cell in your body. Your entire body becomes bathed in, while simultaneously pulsating with, this purifying light. Spiritual energy sets things right; as you begin to radiate this light, it sets you right. Like a software spellchecker reviewing a document to right the errors, spirit does this on all your levels. Stay in this cosmic tune-up as long as you like.

––––––––––––––––

Happiness at the seventh level is decidedly not personal—it is the joy of creation expressing through you. Awakening to the spiritual level needn't be some detached event in your life that stands out separate and distinct from your everyday world. We want to learn not only how to leave our everyday life and enter into spirit, but also how to infuse spirit into our daily life. It's not just about getting less involved to connect with spirit, it's also about bringing awareness to all of our involvements.

Do what you do with great passion and commitment, but without attachment to outcome. Take it all seriously, but not too seriously. You have a body; you have an ego and a personal identity—at least, you answer to your name. So why not develop them and get involved with your life? Instead of settling for complacency and not risking, get invested in your life and, particularly, in the lives of others. Get invested with full passion, make yourself absolutely vulnerable to life, and when it doesn't work out exactly as you wish—and it often won't—be humble before life's great mysteries. When you are humble and awake, you can still learn and grow, especially from life situations that work out differently than you'd planned.

III.

Beyond

——— *the* ———

Pursuit

INTERDEPENDENT
HAPPINESS

A human being is part of a whole, called by us the "Universe," a part limited in time and space. He experiences himself, his thoughts and feelings, as something separated from the rest—a kind of optical delusion of his consciousness. This delusion is a kind of prison for us, restricting us to our personal desires and to affection for a few persons nearest us. Our task must be to free ourselves from this prison, by widening our circles of compassion to embrace all living creatures and the whole of nature in its beauty.

—ALBERT EINSTEIN,
QUOTED IN *The Tibetan Book of Living and Dying*

They say "Enlightenment is easy on a mountaintop, not so easy in the marketplace," and this we all know to be true. Throughout this book we have negotiated the many pitfalls in the path of individual growth and happiness. As if that were not enough, even one who has mastered personal contentment rides the highs and lows of the emotional state of the greater community. We are social beings, and our happiness is ultimately interdependent with the world in which we live.

I recently had the good fortune to attend a five-day workshop on compassion with His Holiness the Dalai Lama. His message is as utterly clear and simple as his famous quote, "My religion is kindness." He teaches that we must treat each other, and all of life, with compassion if we are to save our world. It starts at home in our relationships and how we raise our children. In the schools, compassion and emotional development should be taught as a key component of the early education curriculum. In the workplace and how we run our businesses, in our religions and how we treat each other's faiths, in every area of life, we should live with compassion— and this would change the world. This is his message.

This simple concept may be enough to change the world, so why not try? Although his teaching is simple, it would require an awakening to the mindset of interdependence: our individual well-being and happiness is interdependent with the happiness and well-being of all others. Such a mindset would require an evolutionary step for humanity. As we can see from our work with energy in this book, humanity has been mired in the self-serving lower chakras. This call for compassionate action is the call for humanity to step up to the heart chakra.

It also echoes what is happening with what we have called the reemergence of the Divine Feminine, and again the call for humanity to awaken to the heart-chakra awareness that all of life is interconnected. We could call this time "Awakening into *we*" as we grow into the awareness of just how interwoven all of our lives are.

Compassion comes from feeling the suffering of others and wanting to alleviate it. Suffering is a heavy word, and many shy away from anything at all connected to suffering for fear of getting pulled down into it. In our personal work with the heart chakra and opening to the emotions of others, we learned to "feel it, bless it, and lay it on the lap of the Divine"—a helpful technique for following through on living with compassion. Be open to the emotions of others, but don't hold on to these feelings; keep them moving through you. Feel the emotions, bless the energy, and then send back love and healing energy.

For us, deciding whether to feel these emotions or not is a bit like a fish deciding whether to get wet—we are all in the same ocean of emotion. Most of us sense a lack of skill at handling our own emotions, so opening up to others and processing their emotions can seem overwhelming. It may be that we are overwhelmed only because we mistakenly identify collective emotions as our own. Still, in learning to skillfully deal with these collective issues that we feel anyway, we awaken to the heart of humanity and compassion is born.

Collectively, our wound is rooted in our lack of understanding the interdependency of all life and, thus far, we have demonstrated a tremendous lack of humanity toward humanity. Chief Sealth (also known as Seattle) reminded us that whatever mankind does to the web of life, he does to himself. We have been acting like cells in the same body fighting each other. Imagine your hand sneaking up and attacking your face! We need our visionaries to help us awaken to a larger understanding of the interconnectedness of all life.

Humanity itself must rise to save humanity. We've been waiting to be saved, when it is likely us who will have to do the saving! My theory is that as we awaken to the heart-chakra level, this widespread conscious awareness of the interconnectedness of all life will lead to the awakening of a higher level of intelligence than we have ever had before.

This process is seen in the developing brain of a fetus growing within its mother's womb. Each of the individual centers of the brain that control various bodily functions develops independently of each other until a sufficient level of complexity is achieved, and then a greater, unifying intelligence emerges from the complexity, uniting all the centers as one brain.

This is the evolutionary step for humanity, to unite together as one global intelligence. Humanity can solve these great puzzles before us, but not simply with our individual minds. Each of us is operating with a mere fraction of the mind's potential and it could be that we only need this minimal amount for our individual lives. The 85 percent of our mind that we are not using is the collective mind, the universal mind of humanity that we are cells of consciousness within, and as we unite with each other, we access that greater global intelligence through our intuition.

Neuroscience has also revealed that the specific centers in the brain for intuition and compassion are butted up next to each other. To stimulate one activates the other as well. Open to your intuition and your compassion will expand. Open to your compassion and your intuition will flourish. Of course the opposite is equally true: if one of the centers of compassion or intuition is not being utilized, the other will lack as well.

Synergy is a process in chemistry when two chemicals come together and their combined effect is greater than "one plus one" would suggest. With synergy, one plus one equals more than two. This happens in good conversations at the mental level when ideas get activated that neither person had before the conversation. This is how to access the unused portion of our brain. We are not going to solve our collective problems with "one plus one equals two" thinking. We need to come together synergistically, activating more of the global brain than was previously drawn on.

The global brain is awakening and is experienced by us as a quickening. To stabilize and align with these growing energy surges, there is probably no greater tool than breath-work. Even the simplest technique of breathing deep into your belly and slowly exhaling for several breaths can have an immediate and beneficial impact on your ability to align with intense energy.

SOLUTION-BASED THINKING

We are plenty aware of our problems, and now we need some solutions—not just a revolution against what isn't working, but a revolution toward what can work. We need to get on board with inventing a healthy way to live together on this planet. That's the puzzle. And the hourglass of extinction is a cruel reminder that the time is now if we're going to pull out of it at all.

William McDonough, coauthor of *Cradle to Cradle,* a visionary architect who designs not only green office buildings but also entire green villages, is offering solutions. The creed for his company captures the heart of the collective nature of our times and sets a high standard. Their creed is *"to love all children, of all species, for all times."** Imagine trying to build a policy for any business or government with this as the creed! This, again, is the message to live from the heart.

THE ENERGY SHIFT

A shift is happening. Whereas in previous eras spiritual vision was cultivated only by a designated elite few, now we are in an era where an awakening in consciousness is occurring in broad sectors of the population. This sense of an energy shift is widespread and there are numerous beliefs as to why it is occurring, but for whatever reason, most people feel some type of acceleration going on.

Ilya Prigogine received the Nobel Prize in chemistry in 1977 for his work with dissipative structures. The principle goes far beyond chemistry: a system will grow, reach critical mass, and then begin to dissolve—and from out of the chaos a higher level of order will emerge. This principle of dissipative structures aptly describes what is going on with our business and social policies, policies that can't adapt to meeting the true needs of the people. Yes, there will be endings—endings of systems that weren't working anyway. And out of that chaos a higher order will emerge.

---

*William McDonough and Michael Braungart, *Cradle to Cradle* (New York: North Point Press, 2002).

This quickening of consciousness is leading to greater intuition for many and to greater anxiety for just as many, depending on how skillfully they are handling it. This increased energy is a doorway to heightened awareness. Breathe into it and ride the wave to engage your intuition, rather than trying to quell the wave, which only creates anxiety.

Humanity in the patriarchal era has been like a beehive without the queen bee—no unifying force. With the awakening of compassion, with reconnecting with the Divine Feminine, we find the unifying force of the path of the heart, and although you can't heal our world, and I can't, perhaps *we* can.

SUGGESTED READING

Adyashanti. *Emptiness Dancing.* Boulder, CO: Sounds True, 2006.

———. *True Meditation.* Boulder, CO: Sounds True, 2006.

Bach, Richard. *Illusions.* New York: Dell, 1977.

Bancroft, Anne. *The Dhammapada.* Rockport, MA: Element, 1997.

Barks, Coleman. *The Essential Rumi.* San Francisco: Harper-Collins, 1995.

Brayshaw, Julia M. *Medicine of Place.* Olympia, WA: Alchemia Publishing, 2007.

Brennan, Barbara Ann. *Hands of Light.* New York: Bantam, 1987.

Brezsny, Rob. *Pronoia Is the Antidote for Paranoia.* Berkeley, CA: Frog, 2005.

Cameron, Julia. *The Artist's Way.* New York: G.P. Putnam's Sons, 1992.

Chadwick, David. *Crooked Cucumber.* New York: Broadway Books, 1999.

Chodron, Pema. *When Things Fall Apart.* Boston: Shambhala, 1997.

Coelho, Paulo. *The Alchemist.* San Francisco: HarperCollins, 1993.

Dalai Lama XIV. *The Power of Compassion.* Translated by Geshe Thupten Jinpa. San Francisco: Thorsons, 1995.

———. *An Open Heart.* Edited by Nicholas Vreeland. Boston: Little, Brown, 2001.

Dyer, Wayne. *There's a Spiritual Solution to Every Problem.* New York: Quill, 2003.

Gibran, Kahlil. *The Prophet.* New York: Knopf, 1993.

Hafiz. *The Gift.* Translated by Daniel Ladinsky. New York: Penguin, 1999.

Hanh, Thich Nhat. *Peace Is Every Step.* New York: Bantam, 1991.

Hawken, Paul. *Blessed Unrest.* New York: Penguin, 2008.

Hawkins, David. *Power vs. Force.* Carlsbad, CA: Hay House, 1995.

Judith, Anodea. *Wheels of Life.* St. Paul, MN: Llewellyn, 1997.

Kornfield, Jack. *After Ecstasy, the Laundry.* New York: Bantam, 2001.

Krishnamurti, Jiddu. *Think on These Things.* New York: HarperCollins, 1989.

Long, Max Freedom. *The Secret Science at Work.* Marina del Rey, CA: DeVorss & Co., 1953.

McDonough, William, and Michael Braungart. *Cradle to Cradle.* New York: North Point Press, 2002.

Mipham, Sakyong. *Ruling Your World.* New York: Morgan Road, 2005.

Mitchell, Stephen. *Tao Te Ching.* New York: HarperPerennial, 1992.

Moore, Thomas. *Care of the Soul.* New York: HarperCollins, 1992.

Mortenson, Greg, and David Oliver Relin. *Three Cups of Tea.* New York: Penguin, 2006.

Myss, Caroline. *Anatomy of Spirit.* New York: Harmony, 1996.

Nisargadatta, Maharaj. *I Am That.* Durham, NC: Acorn Press, 1973.

Osborne, Arthur. *Ramana Maharshi and the Path of Self Knowledge.* York Beach, ME: Samuel Weiser, 1970.

Osho. *The Book of Secrets.* New York: Harper & Row, 1977.

Pond, David. *Chakras for Beginners.* St. Paul, MN: Llewellyn, 1999.

———. *Astrology & Relationships.* St. Paul, MN: Llewellyn, 2001.

Reps, Paul, and Nyogen Senzaki. *Zen Flesh, Zen Bones.* Tokyo: Tuttle Publishing, 1957.

Rinpoche, Sogyal. *The Tibetan Book of Living and Dying.* New York: HarperSanFrancisco, 1994.

Roach, Geshe Michael. *The Diamond Cutter.* New York: Doubleday, 2000.

Rodegast, Pat, and Judith Stanton. *Emmanuel's Book.* New York: Bantam, 1989.

Suzuki, Shunryu. *Zen Mind, Beginner's Mind.* New York: Weatherhill, 1970.

Tolle, Eckhart. *A New Earth.* New York: Plume, 2006.

———. *The Power of Now.* Novato, CA: New World Library, 2004.

Trungpa, Chogyam. *Shambhala: The Sacred Path of the Warrior*. Boston: Shambhala, 1984.

Villoldo, Alberto, and Erik Jendresen. *The Four Winds*. New York: Harper & Row, 1990.

Watts, Alan. *Tao: The Watercourse Way*. New York: Pantheon, 1975.

Yogananda, Paramahansa. *Autobiography of a Yogi*. New York: Philosophical Library, 1946.

Free Catalog

Get the latest information on our body, mind, and spirit products! To receive a **free** copy of Llewellyn's consumer catalog, *New Worlds of Mind & Spirit,* simply call 1-877-NEW-WRLD or visit our website at www.llewellyn.com and click on *New Worlds.*

LLEWELLYN ORDERING INFORMATION

Order Online:
Visit our website at www.llewellyn.com, select your books, and order them on our secure server.

Order by Phone:
- Call toll-free within the U.S. at 1-877-NEW-WRLD (1-877-639-9753). Call toll-free within Canada at 1-866-NEW-WRLD (1-866-639-9753)
- We accept VISA, MasterCard, and American Express

Order by Mail:
Send the full price of your order (MN residents add 6.5% sales tax) in U.S. funds, plus postage & handling to:

Llewellyn Worldwide
2143 Wooddale Drive, Dept. 978-0-7387-1403-5
Woodbury, MN 55125-2989

Postage & Handling:
Standard (U.S., Mexico, & Canada). If your order is:
$24.99 and under, add $3.00
$25.00 and over, FREE STANDARD SHIPPING

AK, HI, PR: $15.00 for one book plus $1.00 for each additional book.

International Orders (airmail only):
$16.00 for one book plus $3.00 for each additional book

Orders are processed within 2 business days.
Please allow for normal shipping time. Postage and handling rates subject to change.

Chakras for Beginners

*A Guide to Balancing
Your Chakra Energies*

DAVID POND

The chakras are spinning vortexes of energy located just in front of your spine and positioned from the tailbone to the crown of the head. Blocks or restrictions in their energy flow expresses itself as disease, discomfort, lack of energy, fear, or an emotional imbalance. By acquainting yourself with the chakra system, how they work and how they should operate optimally, you can perceive your own blocks and restrictions and develop guidelines for relieving entanglements.

With *Chakras for Beginners,* you will discover what is causing any imbalances, how to bring your energies back into alignment, and how to achieve higher levels of consciousness.

978-1-56718-537-9
192 pp., 5³⁄₁₆ x 8 $11.95

Spanish edition:
Chakras para principiantes
978-1-56718-536-2 $12.95

Real Steps to Enlightenment
Dynamic Tools to Create Change

Amy Elizabeth Garcia

Connecting with the divine is crucial for spiritual advancement, but choosing a spiritual path is anything but easy.

Amy Elizabeth Garcia simplifies the journey to enlightenment into thirty-three spiritual goals, such as finding your life purpose, developing trust in the universe, relinquishing the need to control, recognizing synchronicity, and fostering peace. Focusing on a specific spiritual lesson, each chapter begins with a divine message from the author's spiritual master that includes stories from his human incarnations. Garcia goes a step further in bringing these concepts to life by sharing her own life experiences. Every chapter includes a prayer inspired by angels and exercises for spiritual growth—the perfect complement to this beginner's guide to enlightenment.

978-0-7387-0896-6
264 pp., 5³⁄₁₆ x 8 $14.95

Authentic Spirituality
The Direct Path to Consciousness

RICHARD N. POTTER

Our world is plagued with problems related to religions that are based on cultural and historical factors. Many people hunger for a practical and reasonable approach to spirituality that does not insult their intelligence. In other words, they are ready for an authentic spirituality of consciousness.

Lifelong mystic Richard Potter explores consciousness-based spiritual paths and demonstrates how the experience of direct mysticism can help you to open your heart and live a life of clarity, joy, peace, and love. Experiment with practices such as meditation, breathwork, sounding, and retreats.

978-0-7387-0442-5
264 pp., 6 x 9 $15.95

x

Gifts of the Soul
Experience the Mystical in Everyday Life

CONSTANCE RODRIGUEZ, PH.D.

Personal transformation and spiritual evolution await you in the mystical realms of the universe. Blending ancient mystery traditions, Jungian psychology, and cutting-edge science, this practical guide is your boarding ticket to soul awareness and inner wisdom.

Psychotherapist Constance Rodriguez shares sacred keys for accessing the elemental, physical, astral, imaginal, and cosmic realms. She introduces the subtle energy body—the personal human energy field linked to the soul—that takes you to these gateways of higher consciousness. Through Dr. Rodriguez's psychonoetic or "soul-knowing" exercises, you can seek guidance from past lives, nature spirits, the four directions, spirit guides, and your own body and imagination. The answers and insights found in these inner and outer worlds can help you heal past trauma, resolve everyday problems, develop intuition, grow spiritually, and understand the path of your soul.

978-0-7387-1311-3
240 pp., 6 x 9 $15.95

Sail into Your Dreams

8 Steps to Living a More Purposeful Life

KAREN MEHRINGER

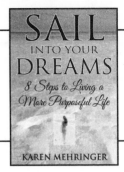

Sail into Your Dreams is the perfect book for anyone who's ever asked, "Is this all there is to life?"

Unsatisfied with her busy life in Seattle, Karen Mehringer embarked on a six-month, life-changing ocean odyssey to Australia, Indonesia, Fiji, and, most importantly, toward the joyful, fulfilling life she had always wanted.

You don't have to leave land to make your dreams come true. Karen shares the wisdom and practical tools she learned on her ocean odyssey, showing us how to focus on what truly matters. Journal entries and inspiring stories from Karen and others highlight how to slow down, nurture yourself, connect with others, and tap into your life force energy—the source of infinite possibilities.

This eight-step program will help you assess your life and eliminate toxic relationships, emotional trauma, physical clutter, and debt—making space for new experiences that awaken your passion and spirit.

978-0-7387-1053-2
240 pp., 5 x 7 $13.95

TO WRITE TO THE AUTHOR

If you wish to contact the author or would like more information about this book, please write to the author in care of Llewellyn Worldwide and we will forward your request. Both the author and publisher appreciate hearing from you and learning of your enjoyment of this book and how it has helped you. Llewellyn Worldwide cannot guarantee that every letter written to the author can be answered, but all will be forwarded. Please write to:

David Pond
c/o Llewellyn Worldwide
2143 Wooddale Drive, Dept. 978-0-7387-1403-5
Woodbury, MN 55125-2989, U.S.A.

Please enclose a self-addressed stamped envelope for reply,
or $1.00 to cover costs. If outside U.S.A., enclose
international postal reply coupon.

Many of Llewellyn's authors have websites with additional information and resources. For more information, please visit our website at:

www.llewellyn.com